A Place Called Braverly

Praise for *A Place Called Braverly*

I am always looking for people to live courageously–no matter how imperfect their courage might be. In Kristy and Kate, I see two people who lead by example, choosing to "live brave, dream bravely, and influence bravery." I have been to Braverly in Mae Sot, Thailand, and I have seen the courageous women who inspired all of this. There's nothing quite like a group of women who find the bravery they need to step into their divine callings as daughters of God. In *A Place Called Braverly*, you will meet this courage head on and will find the strength you need to choose bravery every day.

—**Jessica Honegger**, Founder & Co-CEO, Noonday Collection and Author, *Imperfect Courage*

In *A Place Called Braverly*, Kate and Kristy speak as warm, engaging, and wise friends, encouraging us to dream courageously and audaciously as we lean into the Father's love for us. Through beautifully interwoven personal stories and Scripture passages, you'll come away feeling like you know the authors and, even more importantly, their Father more deeply than you did before. What a gift!

—**Peter Greer**, President and CEO, HOPE International

This is a joyful and inspiring book bursting with stories that feature two who have been on a wonderful journey with Jesus into the world. You will feel that you're best friends with Kate and Kristy as they share from their hearts and reflect on lessons learned along the way. The joy they possess is obvious and this book encourages us all to live more "braverly" as we follow Jesus.

—**Terry Linhart**, Ph.D., Author, *The Self-Aware Leader*
and *Global Youth Ministry*

A Place Called Braverly is no ordinary book for women. It's one of those books that can totally change your life! Kate and Kristy have written a transparent book that will breathe courage into your life, inspire you to follow Jesus wholeheartedly, and challenge you not to be ruled by fear or insecurity.

—**"Biz"**, Founder, Unusual Soldiers
and Author, *Dangerous*

This book will capture the hearts of women of all ages around the globe. *A Place Called Braverly* is written by two women who were challenged to listen to and follow the call of God in their lives, leading them to dream courageously and live bravely. Their journey took them to becoming close friends with women living in very difficult and oppressive situations at a physical place called Braverly in Thailand. There, Kate and Kristy realized a common thread ran through all of their lives. As women, they all dealt with similar issues such as shame, doubt, anxiety, loneliness, and the need for community. Each chapter of *A Place Called Braverly* contains one of their own moving stories told with openness and vulnerability, followed by a biblical teaching that parallels their stories. The reader is encouraged to pause, reflect, and courageously find ways to break through places that need healing and direction in her own life. This book beautifully shares stories of the lavish love God has for each beloved person He has created.

—**Marylou Habecker**, Former First Lady,
Taylor University

Some people talk about doing important things for the Lord. They often excel in expounding theory but come up short in action. That's not my friends Kate and Kristy. They are doers. They have taken and are continuing to take courageous steps in the frontlines of ministry. Their writing is not from untested theories but from a heart of experience—experiences of walking into the hard places and being led by the Holy Spirit in those hard places. Their love of the Lord and deep desire to see others discover the Father's heart is seen on every page. What God is doing for them is what God wants to do for each of us. Through their vulnerable storytelling and powerful Scripture, you too can find the courage to take your own brave steps toward a place that's called "Braverly!"

—**Pastor Dave Engbrecht**, Board Chairman,
World Gospel Mission and Senior Pastor,
Nappanee Missionary Church

The story of *A Place Called Braverly* is about the journey of brave people doing impossible things. The authenticity and vulnerable openness of the authors helps the reader embrace the possibilities in walking out life as followers of Jesus. The motto of bravery is exemplified through the stories of these two. As you read about the trials and victories shared as testimonies, you will find encouragement and strength to continue your personal journey. This book will stir up courage within you to live bravely. This is a must read for anyone wanting to live life bravely and accomplish great things for the Lord.

—**Sharon Williams**, Founder and Director, Act 4 the Nations, Women Alive, and DAWN program

Few things refresh my soul and remind me of the heart of God more than slowing down, hearing the story of others' journey with Jesus, and visiting God's people in other parts of the world. My visit inside these pages of *A Place Called Braverly* with two ladies I love dearly accomplished all three of these, and it was just what my soul needed. I am confident that you will find the refreshment and renewal you need as you encounter *A Place Called Braverly*.

—**Derry Prenkert**, Student Ministry Pastor, Southeast Christian Church and Podcast Host, *My Third Decade*

Kate and Kristy have written a stunning combination of memoir and devotional filled with wisdom far beyond their years. And that's just part of the beauty of it—that women of all ages can draw from this book lessons in strength and courage and, yes, being brave. It's about being brave enough to accept who you are and trust God to fill out His plan in your life. From showing deep transparency in their lives to offering solid Bible messages to asking the reader to pause and reflect at the end of each chapter, Kate and Kristy will challenge you to deeper faith and bravery to take on the life to which God is calling you—and only you.

—**Linda K. Taylor**, Assistant Professor/ Professional Writing, Taylor University

A Place Called Braverly is an elegantly woven tapestry of Kristy and Kate's personal journeys, clearly hard-won cross-cultural understanding, and fresh insights into Scripture—all against a backdrop of missions on the Thailand and Burma border with marginalized women. This book is a must-read for women who are seeking to live life more fully, more bravely, and with more freedom in the Spirit than ever before.

—**Juliet November**, Author, *Honor/Shame Cultures: A Beginner's Guide to Cross-Cultural Missions*

A PLACE CALLED Braverly

A DARE TO LIVE COURAGEOUSLY, DREAM BOLDLY, AND INFLUENCE BRAVERY

KATE BERKEY & KRISTY MIKEL

Inspired by Braverly

NASHVILLE

NEW YORK • LONDON • MELBOURNE • VANCOUVER

A PLACE CALLED **Braverly**

Daring to Live Courageously, Dream Boldly and Influence Bravery

Published in New York, New York, by Morgan James Publishing. Morgan James is a trademark of Morgan James, LLC. www.MorganJamesPublishing.com

Proudly distributed by Ingram Publisher Services.

Morgan James BOGO™

A **FREE** ebook edition is available for you or a friend with the purchase of this print book.

CLEARLY SIGN YOUR NAME ABOVE

Instructions to claim your free ebook edition:
1. Visit MorganJamesBOGO.com
2. Sign your name CLEARLY in the space above
3. Complete the form and submit a photo of this entire page
4. You or your friend can download the ebook to your preferred device

ISBN 9781631958007 paperback
ISBN 9781631958014 ebook
Library of Congress Control Number: 2021920822

Cover Design by:
Rachel Lopez
www.r2cdesign.com

Interior Design by:
Chris Treccani
www.3dogcreative.net

Morgan James is a proud partner of Habitat for Humanity Peninsula and Greater Williamsburg. Partners in building since 2006.

Get involved today! Visit MorganJamesPublishing.com/giving-back

For the women who make Braverly what it is. You constantly show us how to live brave, dream bravely, and influence bravery.

Contents

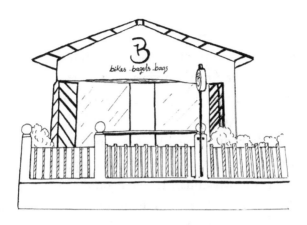

Introduction

By Kristy Mikel and Kate Berkey

This began as so many things do—a simple idea, a spark, a lingering question. That question was simple—what if the trajectory of an entire family's future could change through empowering, training, and investing in women? Braverly, a coffee shop and sewing center, emerged from this and other similar questions. But more than that, it came from a burning passion and dream of its founder, Kayla Koontz.

Kayla is the first to assure you she's not the hero of this story. She doesn't hold a fancy degree or years of business experience. Her expertise—however small it may be—comes from years of trial and error. She's not a savior or the solution. Instead, her beautiful relationship with Jesus sets her apart. Her love from Him and for Him overflows onto those around her. And she desires for families, communities, and whole countries to step closer to the heart of the Father through those who can often go overlooked.

Since Braverly opened its doors in 2016, our mission has been to empower women from oppressed people groups on the Myanmar/Thailand border, to move past their fears and walk in confidence and truth. Time and time again, the Father has far exceeded our dreams, using this idea and mission to continue the work He's already been doing in these women's lives.

Simply put, Braverly is a place that trains women in culinary and sewing skills. In the café, our women make incredible coffee, tea, bagels, salads, and more. They make customers feel at home and learn more customer service skills every day. In the sewing center, our women design bags, headbands, and clutches that reflect their personalities and cultures. They stitch together their ideas and designs, creating beautiful products sold in Thailand and the US.

More than this work and training, Braverly exists to draw women closer to the heart of the Father. We believe Jesus modeled a kind of wholeness of heart everyone can and should experience. So we don't just train our women to do a job or grow in their skills. We strive to show them the person of Jesus Christ and help them develop their own relationship with Him.

Each day in the café, we see the challenge to "Live brave. Dream bravely. Influence bravery." It's the slogan painted across our wall. By this, we mean that fear won't stop us. We won't let fear keep us from trying to learn new things. Fear doesn't stop us from dreaming with the Lord and saying, "Wherever you want me to go and whatever you want me to do, I'll do!" We won't let fear win.

Chewa's Story

Like so many from Myanmar, Chewa grew up knowing firsthand the horrors of the country's military junta. Her family confronted hardship and struggle head on as they spent months at a time escaping the violence which rocked her village. This resilient woman didn't have just one home. Her home was in the jungles of Myanmar and in Mae La refugee camp in Thailand. It was in the refugee camp—a place so far from her village and filled with new kinds of hardships—that she dared to dream about a hopeful, vibrant, beautiful future.

Chewa was one of Braverly's first employees. When Kayla met her, they bonded almost instantly and experienced a kind of immediate sisterhood. Even with her responsibilities as a wife and a mom, Chewa still poured so much time and energy into the café because she believed in this place. She believed it was unique compared to all the other coffee shops in town. Here, she had purpose and value and could help build a place which would impact future generations.

Months after Chewa began working at Braverly, Kayla discovered her friend's silent dream. All those years ago in Mae La refugee camp, Chewa had dreamed of becoming a baker. She imagined making cookies and cupcakes for her family, baking food for her neighbors, and feeding those around her. And at Braverly, Chewa was managing all baked goods, and we were in awe of the Father. Through this simple café, He fulfilled the dream He'd put inside of His beloved daughter so many years ago.

Today, Chewa is a mother of three beautiful girls. She and her husband run a children's home for kids from Myanmar, and she continues to bake for Braverly. She tries new things, even though she might make mistakes. She bakes for her friends and coworkers and for her community. She nourishes those around her, not just with food, but with her joy and life.

But more than this, Chewa is setting an example for her daughters. Every day, she models moving past fear, living with bravery, and dreaming bravely. Because of this, her life sparks bravery in those around her, especially in her family's next generation. Chewa is part of a cultural shift, a beautiful change, not to become more like Kayla but to become the person the Father always designed her to be.

Living with a beautiful wholeness of heart, Chewa knows who she is and whose she is; she knows what the Father says about her, and she knows she belongs to Him. She is a woman who lives in the overflowing love of Jesus. He was already doing a good work inside of our sweet Chewa. We are just blessed to know her, walk through life with her, and help her grow in confidence and truth.

This is what we get to do with these incredible women at Braverly—warriors, resilient fighters, bakers, baristas, and seamstresses. We walk with each other on our journey to wholeness and truth. We challenge one another to move past fear and walk in confidence and truth—each day striving to live out that slogan painted on the wall: Live brave. Dream bravely. Influence bravery.

You are Braverly

This idea and dream is so much bigger than a physical space in Mae Sot, Thailand. It's bigger than our Thai, Karen, Burmese, and American women. You are Braverly as much as Chewa is, because you are a woman of immeasurable value, worth, and influence who is seeking truth and wholeness of heart.

At Braverly, we live and breathe a simple motto of bravery. We live bravely in the routine and risks of each day. We dream bravely beyond our limits for ourselves, our family, our community, our country, and our world. And we encourage bravery in others as we follow Jesus.

It's a daily decision for us, and it's a daily decision you can make too.

Friend, we wholeheartedly believe Jesus created you to embrace this kind of life. He created you to thrive in the gifts He's given you. The Father longs to empower you to live boldly as His daughter every day.

Who is this Father?

We each come to this journey at a different spot, so before we begin, here's what you need to know about what we believe and where we're going. We believe that our heavenly Father God created us with purpose and designed us with unique passions. Each day, He calls us to walk with Him into a life transformed by grace—bravely stepping into our place as daughters in His Kingdom.

Each of us carries the burden of sin, guilt, and shame, and no amount of personal striving can make us the person the Father designed us to be.[1] Because of His great love for us, the Father sent His only Son, Jesus Christ, to die on the cross and pay the debt we could not pay for our sin.[2]

Through Christ who died for us while we were still sinners, we receive the choice to accept the gift of grace, forgiveness, and eternal life. And when we believe with our hearts and confess with our mouths that Jesus is Lord, we will receive the privilege of standing in the place the Father has prepared for us as His sons and daughters.[3]

As members of His family, the Father created us to make known the name of Jesus and to use our dreams, gifts, and passions to make disciples of every nation.[4] Each day, the Father invites us to help transform the world through His grace, truth, and unconditional love.[5]

And we believe that if you've never accepted and chosen to believe He has called you His son/daughter whom He loves without condition, the place for you to begin is in accepting the love, grace, and life Jesus offers. If this is you, we encourage you to pause and jump to the back of the book where you'll find more resources on your journey to the Father. Perhaps you're not ready to make this decision. We understand that and would encourage you to keep reading this book anyway. The Father whom you will read about in these pages is not out of reach. He promises that as we seek Him, we will find Him.[6] He is real and personal, and He is ready to step into a relationship with you whenever you are.

How to Read This Book

Friend, we will walk this journey together. In these pages, you will read stories of our interactions with the Father and with Scripture. We believe that you will find encouragement, hope, and truth in them, and step by step, we trust that the Father will lead you into a greater depth of relationship with Him.

At the end of each chapter, you'll see the section we like to call "The Pause." Every good song needs a pause—when the melody hangs in the air for a moment, when all the musicians can catch their breath, and when the listener can absorb the beauty they've just heard. This is the reason for these sections. As we read stories and interact with Scripture in each chapter, we need to pause. We need to take a break. We need to absorb what we've just read. Otherwise, we risk racing past the moments, stories, and lessons the Father longs for us to learn and absorb.

In these sections, you can reflect on and respond to questions. We encourage you to do whatever helps you process the chapter. For both of us, this means writing our thoughts and prayers in a notebook. Over the years, we've revisited these journals because they remind us of the work the Father has done in our lives. Sometimes, though, it's good to try something new. So, you may encounter promptings to paint, draw, or go on a walk. You might want to try these things, even if they seem unusual. They just might help you discover a new way to connect with Jesus.

We experience life to the fullest when we do it with others. We created this journey for your community, your friends, and your family. So process however you need to on your own, but then step into your community. Share with one another in honesty, vulnerability, and courage. Don't be afraid to admit your struggles or the lies you believe. Chances are, others around you face similar struggles. The Father created us to do this life in community, so let's practice that togetherness.

You are Loved

Friend, before we begin, we want you to know that you are loved. The Father sees you and knows you. He holds you in the highest honor and gives you the greatest value out of all creation. You bring so much to the table—your gifts and talents, your ideas and opinions, your stories and thoughts. You belong here, and we are so grateful you came.

Together, let's go on this journey.

The Pause

A Prayer for the Journey

Father, you created us for courage, embedded it into our
    DNA.

May we be women who believe this truth.

You designed us to live brave, to choose courage over fear
    in our living and breathing.

May we be women who boldly choose this way of life.
You crafted us to dream bravely, to reach beyond our own
ability and take your hand.
May we be women who imagine impossible, Kingdom
sized dreams.
You called us to influence bravery, to lock arms with others
and walk in boldness together.
May we be women whose lives and dreams send ripples of
bravery into our community.

Teach us to take this step by step, trusting you with the
journey.
Teach us to bring all we are–our whole story, our joys, our
pains, our dreams that feel dead.
Teach us to invite others into our journey, choosing
vulnerability over isolation.
Teach us to anchor ourselves to who You are, believing the
truths You sing over our lives.

Give us grace for the steps forward and back.
Give us grace for the moments we get it right and the
moments we wish we could forget.
Give us grace for our humanity, our imperfections, our
failing and falling.

You love us. Thank you.
You walk with us. Thank you.
You dream with us. Thank you.
You believe in us. Thank you.

Father, with each step, take us into lives marked by courage.

Your Own Prayer for the Journey

This is our prayer for you and this journey, but the Father longs to hear your battle cry. So, before we take another step, write a prayer for your journey into a life marked by courage. Write it in a journal or in the space below with words or pictures. Shout it at the top of your lungs or whisper it to an empty room. Share it with someone you love. Do whatever you need to let it settle over your spirit. Then, let's walk through these pages together.

Chapter 1

Resting in the Father's Extravagant Love

By Kate Berkey

Running in a Losing Race

"I can't do this anymore" I said as tears zigzagged down my dirt-crusted face.

I lifted my head from the ground, begging the finish line to be just ahead, but all I could see was more of the trail—dirt and mud and rocks poking above the ground. My heart rate wasn't slowing down, and I couldn't seem to catch my breath. It was as if all of the oxygen had been sucked out *of the world, and I was left trying to breathe air unfit for humans.*

My body—weary and worn—ached to lay on the ground a little longer. Surely I could catch my breath then. If I could just take a quick break, I could keep running. And soon, I could finish the race.

But my heart and mind told my legs to do what they could not. "Get up. You're behind. You're so weak. Look at everyone else. They're doing just fine. Why can't you keep up with them? Be better, faster. Be stronger than this. Keep running."

And so I did.

I picked my weary bones up out of the dirt and wiped the tears from my eyes. With one foot in front of the other, I kept running. Not that I knew where I was going. Not that I knew where the finish line was.

But I ran, and I ran hard. Because it's easier to ignore brokenness when life just keeps moving.

This Road Called Proving

I don't think I'm the only one who's been here—broken, exhausted, stuck on a road that seems to have no end. It's the road called striving. Maybe some call it working. I know it as "proving," and I've struggled to find a different way my entire life.

We know what this road is like, right? With the constant refrain, "You're not good enough" ringing in our ears, we try to earn love and acceptance and belonging. But there's a catch to this road. It has no end. There are no breaks. There is no finish line. We cannot win no matter how hard we try.

And it's completely exhausting.

In May 2017, I found myself wrapped up in an intense season of proving—sprinting down a road that led nowhere. In this season, a bunch of great things kept me running at a pace I couldn't maintain. My friends, family, and the man I planned to marry took most of my time. Outside of that, I served at my local church and worked long hours at my job in full-time ministry. Through all of this doing, I tried to prove to everyone around me that I was strong and capable and could handle anything. Deep within my spirit, though, I was trying to prove that I belonged and was worthy of love and acceptance.

All this striving exhausted my body, and I wondered with an aching heart if any of it mattered. My body was bloated, and I struggled to turn my mind off at night. My anxious heart and quick tongue snapped at those I loved the most. This version of Kate scared me, but I felt trapped. So, on a rainy spring weekend, I gave myself permission to ask the questions that lingered in my mind and to write what was on my heart, even the ugliest words. For hours, I filled pages in my journal with thoughts about working, earning, and proving, asking questions that didn't seem to have answers.

If I was doing good things for Jesus, why did I feel so empty? Why was I so tired? Was I really doing things that mattered? How could I get off this road called proving? When would the striving end? Would I ever prove to myself and to others that I was worthy, I belonged, I was good enough?

While writing, the Father whispered to my soul, "The opposite of proving is resting in My extravagant love."

I hesitated before writing His words in my journal because it seemed too good to be true and definitely unattainable. Two years and one failed relationship later, I boarded an airplane and moved 9,000 miles from home. And it was here, after years of struggle, that I encountered the story of a father running down a road to his child, and I inhaled my Father's extravagant love for the first time. Here, I found a place of rest.

The Story of the Prodigal's Father

Moving to a new place—especially one of a different culture—certainly provides a new perspective. Familiar and normal things disappear, and suddenly everything is new. As someone who grew up in the church, I'm also realizing how valuable new and different perspectives are for the stories I've heard a hundred times.

I'm not saying that long-standing truths should be thrown out the window—exchanged for something new and shiny. That's a truly dangerous way to approach Scripture. But sometimes, when stories and songs and wise sayings become old friends, we need to look at them in a way that leads us into greater understanding.

Personally, as I study, the Bible comes alive through different translations—New International Version, The Message, King James Version, The Passion Translation. I see the ways they build upon one another, inviting me deeper and deeper into their familiar stories. For me, the story of the prodigal son came alive when I read it in The Passion Translation of the Bible. It's language and the emotion that dripped off the page placed me in the story and allowed me to experience it as if I was the prodigal himself. For the first time, it wasn't the tale of a rebellious teenager. It was much deeper and more beautiful than I had ever known.

This is the story of a father and his two sons. The younger son, in total disregard for his dad, asks for his inheritance. What a slap in the face. Nothing says, "You're better dead than alive," than this. Despite the audacity of this request, the father obliges and gives him the money.

The son moves far away and wastes it all. With nothing left and facing starvation, he takes a job at a farm feeding the pigs. Only when he eats some of their slop does he realize he doesn't have to live this way. Even the servants in his father's house have it better. He decides to return home and beg, not for his place in the family, but for a job as the family's servant.

What happens next is the extravagant, over-the-top love that shook me to my core.

> So the young son set off for home. From a long distance away, his father saw him coming, dressed as a beggar, and great compassion swelled up in his heart for his son who was returning home. The father raced out to meet him, swept him up in his

arms, hugged him dearly, and kissed him over and over with tender love.

Then the son said, "Father, I was wrong. I have sinned against you. I could never deserve to be called your son. Just let me be—"

The father interrupted and said, "Son, you're home now!"

Turning to his servants, the father said, "Quick, bring me the best robe, my very own robe, and I will place it on his shoulders. Bring the ring, the seal of sonship, and I will put it on his finger. And bring out the best shoes you can find for my son. Let's prepare a great feast and celebrate. For my beloved son was once dead, but now he's alive! Once he was lost, but now he is found!" And everyone celebrated with overflowing joy.

Luke 15:20-24, TPT

Let's Get Some Context

Every time I read this story now, it takes my breath away, but for years, I missed its beauty—the extravagant love of the father. I blame it on my western context. Scripture wasn't written from my cultural perspective. In fact, nothing is more opposite than my American life. It wasn't until I was totally immersed in Thailand's honor and shame culture—which almost mirrors that of Jesus' day—that I began to understand the nuances of this story.

Not long after arriving in Mae Sot, I learned the high value placed on honor and absolute disdain for shame. Before I moved here, I thought I was someone who showed the proper amount of respect and honor to others, but I soon realized that my actions were a fraction of what this culture expected. While everyone around me bowed toward one another as a sign of respect, I stood still. When people kept their feet covered, I stuck them straight out, essentially flipping off those in the room. And let me just say that there's nothing like accidentally flipping off people in a church service. That will teach you cultural norms quickly! My life was filled with a dozen little mistakes, each reminding the Thais around me that I was a foreigner who didn't understand what honor and shame meant in this culture. For months, I fumbled and stumbled, becoming the farang (that white person) Thais shook their heads at.

I had so much to learn—not only about how to show respect, but also about who received the highest respect. In the family, this person was the father. He is the defender of the family, protector of their honor. Holding the most authority and respect, his opinion outweighs all others. Women, no matter their age, have to ask their father or husband for permission and advice on nearly every area of life. Families don't decide on anything without the father's input, because it's his job to avoid shame at all costs. In my American culture, "saving face" is simply a phrase. In Mae Sot, it's life.

Because of my cultural misunderstanding in the story of the prodigal son, I missed the most important character, the one who changes everything—the father. The main character isn't the son who left or the brother who stayed. This is a story about a father who created space in his family for both—even honoring the one who had brought the deepest kind of shame to them all. Instead of protecting himself, the father heaps burning coals of shame on his own head.

The father waits and watches. He strains his eyes day after day to look for his son, the one who dishonored him and his family in the worst of ways. When the father sees his son a long distance away, his overwhelming love and compassion compels him to run toward, not away from, his son. He gives little care to his garments, uncovering his legs so he can sprint.[7] Although you and I might not see the big deal in showing a little skin, this was incredibly shameful in this culture.

Arms wide open, he takes the boy in his arms and lavishes him with love, kissing him over and over again. This shocking display of emotions was reserved for women; men were expected to suppress their feelings, locking them deep within their heart. But this outrageous outpouring leaves no questions—the father loves his son.

Instead of slipping home unnoticed, the father throws an over-the-top party in honor of the one who dishonored him, welcoming his son home for everyone to see. He doesn't care about saving face. He invites the entire community as if it were a long-awaited "Welcome Home" party rather than the shameful return of a shameful son.

With every move he makes, the father takes on the humiliation reserved for his son. He changes everything.

He uproots all our preconceived notions about love, grace, forgiveness, honor, and shame.

Do you see it? Jesus showed us another way. He gave us a glimpse of our heavenly Father's extravagant, over-the-top love, and until we can see and experience it, we may never find the rest and courage we long for.

Cutting a Ceremony Short

As I uncovered more context around the story of the prodigal, I learned about a custom that caused me to pause—the kezazah ceremony.[8] Everyone listening to Jesus tell this story would have been waiting for justice, for the son to get what he deserved. But it's not there.

It was a familiar custom, one some in the crowd may have experienced in their community. In it, a Jewish son who had dishonored his family was cut off from everyone—his family, friends, and entire community—if he dared to return home. Friends and family dragged him to the middle of the town, and once in the most public part of the community, they broke a pot at his feet, shouting things like, "You are now cut off from your family!"

And that was it. Without a chance to fight for a place in his family or apologize or explain, the community cut him off. When the clay pot shattered at his feet, everyone disowned him. It was as if he was dead, crushed by the weight of shame. Like the tiny pieces of the pot at his feet, it was impossible to put back together the life, love, and belonging he had once experienced.

The son could do nothing. No amount of work or words could undo what he had done. He couldn't prove or earn or work his way toward belonging, love, or grace. Only a father could redeem his son. So this is why he watched and waited. He strained his eyes, looking for a slim figure on the horizon, and when his son was still far from home, the father ran to reach him before shame could. The father hugged and kissed his son over and over again. The son couldn't even finish his well-rehearsed speech, begging for a job as a servant. He had a place in the family, and it didn't change because of his words or actions. He belonged because he was a son.

In his father's face, the son saw love of the deepest kind, and in his father's actions, the son experienced the highest honor. That day, there was no kezazah ceremony. The son was not crushed by shame. His family did not cut him off. They did not treat him like a slave or servant. He was not an outcast. His father—the one he shamed the most— honored him as the beloved son who dared to walk home.

On a Journey Home to the Father

I was on my own kind of journey home when this story completely overwhelmed me. In the newness and differences of Thailand, I once again found myself on that old road called "Proving." This time, though, I confronted something new—deep, unending shame.

After moving to Mae Sot, I felt lost in transition and culture shock, trying to prove I was good enough to be on a team of incredible people. Still picking up the pieces from a failed relationship with the man I had planned to marry, I felt like I needed to prove I was fine as a strong, independent, single woman even though I mostly felt unsure and insecure. Even in my relationship with the Father, it was as if I was trying to prove I was okay, that my life wasn't out of my control.

I felt weak, exposed, and lost in unfamiliar territory, but more than that, I felt ashamed that I couldn't pull myself out of the pit of shame. Those days, not even the Father's love felt safe. So, I ran away from Him, away from home. I moved down that old road, the one with no end. I kept myself busy, ignoring the One who wanted to embrace me in relationship and honor me even in my brokenness.

I was the prodigal daughter in need of the Father's extravagant love, and as old struggles tried to strangle me, He whispered new words that freed my soul.

I have waited for you—watching for the day, the minute, the moment I saw you on the long, dusty road. I exposed myself so you wouldn't be exposed. I ran so you wouldn't have to run and so shame couldn't catch you. Before a word could escape your lips, I claimed you as my own. You are my daughter, and nothing changes that.

Let me do what is shameful, embarrassing, and ridiculous. Let me do all this to show you just how much I love you. Let me see you from a distance and let me run. Let me hold you and kiss you over and over again. Let me run to you, because I love you.

His words reduced me to tears. More than anything, I needed to believe the Father wanted to run to me, embrace me in my brokenness, fight for me, clothe me as His daughter, and bring me back home. He didn't have to. He wanted to. Because this is who He is.

A Father's Love

Every so often, the Father gives us glimpses of heaven on earth in those around us. As His truth washed over my heart and mind, I thought of a different man, one who had embraced me as his daughter every day of my life—my earthly father. Over and over again, I've found the courage to live past fear in the steadiness of his love. It's a love that gives a place for my fear and doubts to land, a place for peace to cover them. It's a love that says, "I've got you, and you've got this!"

No truer was this than the day I moved to Thailand. That morning, my parents loaded my suitcases in the back of their car, and we drove in silence for much of the two-hour drive to the airport. In the back seat, I tried to swallow my tears and push my fear and questions away. My parents seemed to process in their own way, making business calls or staring out the window. As a woman who hasn't had children yet, I didn't understand what it was like to send your youngest child and only daughter to a country 9,000 miles away. It was difficult, I'm sure. It was the end of a season, a way of life, and a kind of normal. Or maybe it felt like letting go, even if everything in you wanted to cling to your child.

Burned into my memory is the goodbye hug I shared with my dad at the airport. It was the tightest I remember him holding me. I felt like a kid again, like how he must have held me as a baby, making sure I didn't slip from his grasp. He cradled my head as I cried into his neck, soaking his shirt and skin. I was 25 years old, but I wanted my dad to hold and protect me like only a dad can.

In my dad's face that day, I saw a love that left me breathless. It's the kind that protects and wants what's best for the other. It said, "I see you. I know you. I believe in you. I'm here to catch you. So, go." It was a love that sends rather than holds, and I had access to it because I was my father's daughter.

When I think of the prodigal's father, this love comes to mind. That day, I didn't leave my family in the way the son did. In fact, it had nothing to do with my coming or going. It had to do with what I found in my father's love.

His love was extravagant and moving, unashamed of the tears and outpouring of emotion. It disregarded its own image, social norms, and protocols. In it, I found courage. I found belonging. I found rest. I found a place that would catch me if I fell.

This is what we find in the Father's love too. In His perfect love that casts out all fear, we find a place of peace. And from the resting place of His love, we find the life our soul craves—a life overflowing with courage.

The Resting Place of the Father's Extravagant Love

I pray that out of his glorious riches he may strengthen you with power through his Spirit in your inner being, so that Christ may dwell in your hearts through faith. And I pray that you, being rooted and established in love, may have power, together with all the Lord's holy people, to grasp how wide and long and high and deep is the love of Christ, and to know this love that surpasses knowledge—that you may be filled to the measure of all the fullness of God.

Ephesians 3:16-19

Whether or not we realize it, I think most of us are searching for a place of rest, because we're tired of running down those unending roads called striving, working, earning, or proving. On our best days, we might think to look for it in the Father's love. We're like the prodigal, ready to trade our place as daughters in the family of God to be servants in His house. But He has so much more for us. Even in our shame, He creates a place of honor we don't have to work for or earn. We can come to it with confidence, holding up our head instead of hiding our face.

In The Passion Translation, Ephesians 3:17 says that "the life of Christ will be released deep inside you and the resting place of his love will become the very source and root of your life." This, to me, is one of the most incredible truths I've ever encountered in Scripture. There is a rest the Father longs for us to live from. This space really exists. It's not too good to be true. It's there, and it can be the source and root of our lives. Here the Father lavishes us with love, honor, and freedom—things we could never earn no matter how hard we try.

Some days I think back to the girl stuck on that never-ending road of striving—exhausted, worn out, a hollow version of myself. I think about the words the Father whispered to my soul, "the opposite of proving is resting in My extravagant love." These words ushered in a change, a new season, another step deeper into the Father's love. These days, they no longer feel impossible or far-fetched. Instead, they feel freeing—inviting me to disqualify myself from my race to prove and find rest in the Father's abundant love. It's here each of us finds the courage to stare down fear and charge past it toward the place we always knew we should go—a place of deep, steadfast bravery.

Until the resting place of His love is the root of our lives, all our running—even if it looks like brave living—will be little more than attempts to prove ourselves to a Father with whom we have nothing to prove.

So here's my challenge: stop running down the roads with no end. Disqualify yourself from the race to strive and earn, and let the Father run toward you. He longs to honor you, even if you feel you are unworthy of this honor. Let Him reach you before shame can. Let Him lavish His love on you and embrace you as the prodigal. Only He can redeem you and create a perfect place of belonging for you in His family. So let Him lead you home.

The Pause

Here it is, our first Pause. It's the very essence of what we just talked about—a break, a moment of rest. So let's catch our breath and do something you might not have done before. As we embrace The Pause, use the space below or pull out your journal. This is a tool for the journey— something you can come back to months and years from now. When I journal, I write specific Scripture that sticks out to me, words I hear the Father speak, and prayers to Him. You can use your journal in this same way, but don't let my experience limit you. Maybe you want to reflect on this journey by drawing pictures in this book or in your journal or doing other creative things in these pages. This is simply a way for you to connect with the Father, because He longs to speak to you!

So often He speaks through His Word, and reading the Bible is one of the clearest ways we get to interact with Him. We can choose to believe in its truth and its power to transform our lives. So let's sit with its truth for a while, allowing the Holy Spirit to speak to us through words written so very long ago.

I want you to go back and read Luke 15:11-24. As you do, imagine you are the prodigal and God is the father. What sticks out to you as you read it in this way?

Why does this stand out to you?

Now, I want you to imagine you are the prodigal who is a long way from home. You look up and see the Father running to you. What do you imagine His face looks like?

What does He say when He reaches you?

How does His lavish outpouring of extravagant love make you feel?

Here, in this love, we find the courage to live bravely because we know that His love catches us. We can step off the road called "striving" or "proving" or "working" and enter His place of rest. This resting place can be the very source and root of our life—changing the decisions we make, the way we live, the way we let fear affect us.

The prodigal experienced the resting place when the father reminded him who he was. He was not a slave or servant in his father's house. He was a son, and his place in the family changed everything. The same is true for us.

To rest in the Father's love, we need to embrace the name He gives us. And He calls us daughter. So let's take a step further on this journey—redeeming the name He gives us.

Chapter 2

He Calls Me Daughter

By Kristy Mikel

Planting a Lie

"Shoot!" my dad's voice echoed through the house.

It was a sound my sisters and I grew accustomed to on most winter nights as my dad reclined in his armchair shouting to the players on the television. Another basketball season had come, and he took up his usual position of coaching and encouraging the Indiana University Hoosiers from the comfort of our living room—as if the players could hear his words.

My dad loves basketball. At a young age, my sisters and I learned how to dribble and shoot a ball when my dad hung a hoop at the edge of our driveway. We spent countless summer nights shooting baskets and playing games until long after the sun went down. In the winter, we gathered around the television in the living room to watch college teams play and listen to my dad's commentary—a fun tradition that turned into something special shared between our dad and each of us. I loved sharing this time with him and could see how proud it made him.

When I tried out for the school team, my dad was there to cheer me on. He came to nearly every game I played, coaching me from the sidelines or giving me advice on the drive home afterward. He beamed with pride whenever he talked with others about our shared love for the sport. It was our special thing—a way for father and daughter to connect. So when the day came that I didn't want to play anymore, it terrified me to tell my dad. I didn't want to lose the special thing we shared. I didn't want to disappoint him, but I had grown tired of playing the sport. It was time for a break.

As another basketball season approached, I desperately tried to work up the courage to tell my dad I would not play. It felt like I was letting go of something special—like losing the thing that made him proud of me. I didn't realize how much I believed our relationship hinged on my place on the team.

The conversation went okay, but it's not one I remember. The conversation I remember is the one my dad and I never had. Soon after I told him about my decision to quit playing, I overheard him talking to one of his buddies about it.

"She could've been great," he told his friend. These are the words I remember.

My dad meant to compliment me. Had I been standing with him, he likely would've said how proud he was. Sure, he was bummed I was no longer on the team and that he could no longer cheer for me from the sidelines. But he was proud of me, his daughter whom he loved.

But what I heard in his words was a twisted version of the truth—a lie my mind grabbed onto. This lie rooted itself into every part of my life as I struggled to be perfect.

Kristy, you're not good enough, came the lie. These were words he had never spoken, yet ones that tore at the very fabric of my worth.

Distance crept into my relationship with my dad. Like an unwelcome guest, this lie made its home, reframing the relationship my dad and I shared. Believing he saw me as a disappointment, I allowed myself to think I would never fully measure up to the person he wanted me to be. I became frustrated and easily angered whenever I was around him. Gone were the special moments we once shared, and not because he didn't try. They were gone because I stopped believing I was worthy of them.

Years later, I finally allowed myself to revisit the day I overheard my dad's words when I joined my sister at a Bible study. Sitting around a table with a group of strangers, the pastor asked us to think about the words that had been spoken over us—words that defined who we were and what we believed.

"She's not good enough," I scribbled on the paper in front of me.

Tears filled my eyes as I felt the weight of those words. My mind flashed back to the high school version of Kristy overhearing the conversation once again, but as I replayed it in my mind, I heard it differently.

"She could've been great," echoed my dad's voice.

It was the first time I felt like I understood what he meant. Tears now running down my face, I thought about my dad, about the relationship we once had and lost because of my inability to see the truth. I allowed a lie to take root, slowly destroying my relationship with my father. And that night the lie fell apart because I understood it wasn't true.

But as truth tried to take its place, another unwelcome guest made its home in my heart—shame. It washed over me as though wrapping me in a thick, heavy blanket.

"Look at what you've done," shame said. "There's no way to fix it."

I felt so ashamed of how I had treated my dad for years, and I struggled with the shame that said our relationship was beyond repair. I spent years treating my father with subtle disrespect, hurting him for all the ways I believed he hurt me. I was a broken mess.

Honestly, it felt easier to hold onto shame rather than fix what it had broken. It somehow felt safer to sit in the mess I'd created rather than clean it up and risk exposing it to others.

This lie grew for years—its roots tearing apart my self-confidence and identity. I believed for so long I was a disappointment to my dad. I believed I had to work harder, be better, strive more. I believed I wasn't good enough, and the thought of trying to dig this lie out felt exhausting, humiliating even—especially knowing it would mean having a tough conversation with my dad.

As I struggled with the Lord—my heavenly Father—His gentle voice broke through.

"Kristy, I want to redeem your relationship with your dad. I want to redeem your identity of being a daughter."

Redeeming a Daughter

On my journey of redemption, the Lord led me back to a story in Scripture I had read plenty of times before—read but never fully comprehended. It comes from Mark 5:21-34.

It's the story of a woman who bled for twelve years. She suffered a great deal—going to countless doctors, spending all she had in attempts to get better. But for all her efforts, she only got worse. And now mentally, physically, and emotionally exhausted from her constant striving and falling short, this woman came to the end of herself. So when she heard Jesus was passing through her town, she quietly pushed her way through the crowd—desperately trying to reach Him.

Stretching out her hand, she thought, "If I can just touch His clothes I will be healed."

As she grabbed the edge of His garment, her bleeding immediately stopped, and she felt her whole body freed from her suffering.

At once Jesus realized that power had gone out from Him. He turned around in the crowd and asked, "Who touched my clothes?"

"You see the people crowding against you," His disciples answered, "and yet you can ask, 'Who touched me?'"

But Jesus kept looking around to see who had done it. Then the woman, knowing what had happened to her, came and fell at His feet and, trembling with fear, told Him the whole truth. He said to her, "Daughter, your faith has healed you. Go in peace and be freed from your suffering."

Mark 5:30-34

In those days, this woman would have been known as "unclean." She had bled for twelve years without explanation. Doctors couldn't seem to help her, no matter how much money she paid for answers. She had a disease no one understood or could help. She was unclean in every sense of the word.

"Unclean! Unclean!" It's what she was required to yell whenever she walked down the street—a clear warning for people to stay away. She shouldn't have been in the crowd that day. Had people known, they would've cast cursory glances her way. The crowds would split around her—like Moses parting the Red Sea. This woman was unworthy of rubbing shoulders with others. Someone in her condition was supposed to stay far from people—isolated and alone in her suffering.

For twelve years, this is what life taught her.

Stay away. You're not worthy. You are unclean!

With every sideways glance from others, every daily reminder of her disease, every warning cry she needed to shout—her disease became her identity. Sneaking out of her house and down the streets, she slipped into the crowds carefully. She silently pushed her way toward Jesus—trying to remain unnoticed at His back. And trying not to cause a scene, she reached out and touched the back of His robe.

And there it was—a part of the story I never understood before. This woman came behind Jesus because she believed she wasn't worthy of coming before Him. Shame always leaves us in isolation—feeling unworthy of belonging. Dependent on secrecy and fear, shame always leads us to believe we are—and are meant to be—alone.

This woman carried the shame of her disease for twelve years. Only she had felt the weight of it. It was her shame that cut her off from the rest of the world—a giant ravine she could never cross. She not only believed she was alone but that she was meant to be. And this shame stopped her from running before Jesus. Because of shame, she hung her head when He asked who touched Him.

Shame tells us we are alone and convinces us we are meant to stay that way. Shame tells us things will be far worse if we are ever found out.

Not unlike this woman, I believed a lie about myself for years. I carried a name I was never meant to carry—*You are not enough.* Each day I struggled against comparing myself to those around me. If only I was more like her—as smart, as pretty, as outgoing, or as funny—then people would love me. Then people would be impressed by me, proud of me, and the lies go on and on. Shame told me I was alone in the struggle.

"No one else feels the way you do," it whispered.

So I continued to walk with shame—too afraid to step out from behind its shadow.

Speaking to Shame

And then Jesus spoke to shame.

Turning around in a sea of people all pushing, pulling, and bumping into one another just to be near Him, Jesus stopped and looked for the one who had touched Him. Speaking loud enough for everyone to hear, Jesus asked who touched His clothes.

"Jesus, there are so many people crowding around you," His disciples responded, "Everyone is touching you! How can you ask that?"

It was a fair question if Jesus was speaking to the disciples, but He wasn't.

Jesus kept looking around, searching for the one who had touched Him.

He stopped. He waited. He let the question hang in the air, waiting for the one He was speaking to—certain she would respond.

Knowing Jesus was speaking to her, the woman fell before His feet. Head hung low and body shaking, she told the truth of what happened. This woman who tried so hard to stay quiet and unnoticed in the crowd was now the focus of their attention. Jesus called her out, uncovering her to everyone. They expected His reprimand, but as she trembled at His feet, Jesus called her by a name she didn't even know was hers.

"Daughter, your faith has healed you," Jesus said. "Go in peace and be freed from your suffering."

Daughter.

The power of that name in that moment was life changing. Trembling and afraid, face hidden at His feet, she was seen by Jesus, and Jesus called her by name. With one word, Jesus disarmed every lie this woman ever believed about herself. Daughter—a name that told this woman she was not alone. It was a name that called her out of isolation and into her place in the family. Daughter—a name that gave access and authority. She had a place where she belonged—not on the outskirts of town, separated from others, or alone in her suffering. This name made her position clear. She was a daughter, and a daughter belongs in the family.

I didn't realize how much this same word needed redeeming in my life. Just as much as my relationship with my father needed to be redeemed, I needed to relearn who I was.

Part of this relearning meant seeking reconciliation with my dad. I knew the Lord was asking me to take a step and talk with him, yet my shame was so heavy I couldn't bring myself to start the conversation until the day the burden of shame became too much. That day, I paced between the bedroom and kitchen countless times, wiping away my tears with every failed attempt to stop and talk to my dad who sat in the room I passed through.

"Something on your mind?" he asked as I passed by once again.

Tears filled my eyes and my heart raced.

My dad muted the television and leaned forward. Embarrassed and shaking, I sat close to him and spoke.

"Dad, I'm sorry," I mumbled through my tears. "I'm sorry for the way I've been treating you."

My sobs were met with uncomfortable silence. I glanced up to see my dad looking at me—a look of surprise on his face as tears ran down his cheeks. Holding his gaze now, I told him about the conversation I'd overheard all those years ago, about the words I'd thought he said. Through tears, he looked at me and said, "Kristy, I've never been disappointed in you. You're my daughter, and I love you."

My dad spoke to my shame and called me his daughter. Just as Jesus had spoken to the bleeding woman hiding among the crowds: he called her daughter and restored her place for all to see. So too did my father's words crush the lie I carried—casting shame from my mind.

Breathing a heavy sigh of relief, I felt peace fill my heart and mind. Truth took its rightful place over shame. Courage and confidence stepped back into the room as his words soaked into my life.

I was not Kristy, the basketball player.

I was not Kristy, the honor roll student.

I was not Kristy, a good person.

I was Kristy, a daughter—deeply loved and accepted by my father because I belong to him and am part of his family.

Daughter, You Have Access

That conversation with my dad marked a turning point in my journey of not only understanding how he sees me but also how my heavenly Father sees me. For years, I struggled to see God as Father, Papa, Abba—names I heard others use but could never say myself. Years of a strained relationship with my father skewed my understanding. I struggled to see myself as a daughter my heavenly Father was proud of—believing I needed to earn His love and approval, that I had to be worthy of it. All along He was telling me I was His daughter.

Now, I recognize that we come to the table with different experiences with the word *father*. I understand my redemptive journey with my father may not reflect your story. For some, your father has been abusive, distant, or absent. Let me say, my heart aches with you, and I wish I could help change your reality. For all the ways you have felt forgotten, pushed aside, or used, my heart breaks with you. For those who feel a heavy weight from the word father because of something yours said, or you thought he said, my heart aches with you because I know the burden of that weight.

But I can tell you, you are a daughter the Father is proud of and in whom He delights! Your Father in heaven, the One who created you and knows you better than you know yourself, delights in you. He loves you without condition, and He longs to restore your status as a daughter. He longs for you to know your rightful place in His family.

We are His daughters, and that name gives us access. The Scripture speaks of this:

> And you did not receive the "spirit of religious duty," leading you back into the fear of never being good enough. But you have received the "Spirit of full acceptance," enfolding you into the family of God. And you will never feel orphaned, for as He rises up within us, our spirits join Him in saying the words of tender affection, 'Beloved Father!' For the Holy Spirit makes God's fatherhood real to us as He whispers into our innermost being, "You are God's beloved child!"
>
> And since we are His true children, we qualify to share all His treasures, for indeed, we are heirs of God himself. And since we are joined to Christ, we also inherit all that He is and all that He has.
>
> Romans 8:15-17a, TPT

Daughter, you have access to the things the Father has. Just as the woman in Mark 5 had access to the healing power of Jesus because she was His daughter, we have access to all that He is and all that He has to offer! *We have received the Spirit of full acceptance, enfolding us into the family of God!* And we have a Father who is calling us out of our shame, out of our hiding, out of our isolation so we will never feel orphaned again. It is His promise to us to never leave us nor forsake us, to go before us and behind us, to remain with us through the Holy Spirit—the one He left for us to guide us into all truth. We are His daughters, we are enough, and He gives to us all that He has.

Sisters, friends, daughters, it is this access that gives us the courage to live bravely.

As daughters, it is our right to access and walk in freedom over shame. We are no longer isolated, unclean, or cut off. Instead, we have a Father who looks on us with love and full acceptance, lifting the weight of our shame so we can walk confidently with Him. As daughters, it is our right to access and walk in truth over lies—no longer held captive by the words spoken over us by others, words we may have thought we heard. We take captive every thought to make it obedient to Christ.[9] Now we can be filled with the truth of our given name—beloved daughter in whom the Lord delights. As daughters, it is our right to access and walk in confidence over fear. It is because of who He says we are that we can find the courage to live bravely. We do not bow to insecurity. We do not wear a crown of shame. We will not be shaken by the voices who call to us and say we can't, we shouldn't, or we will never be.

We are enough.

We are loved.

We are not alone.

We belong.

We are known.

We are cherished.

We are covered by a Father who cares for and is watching out for our well-being.

He calls to us, "Daughter, my beloved daughter, walk with Me."

The Pause

Daughter, you are enough.

Take a moment to let that hang in the air. Let it soak into your mind, covering any other thoughts or lies. *You are enough.*

Each of us carries words—things spoken to us that have shaped who we are and who we can become. It's time to acknowledge those words. It's time to stack them up against the truth of the Father and allow this truth to take its rightful place. So I want you to use the space below or a journal and go somewhere you won't be interrupted. Close your eyes, take a deep breath, and ask the Lord to reveal to you the words that define you. Maybe they are names that others gave you or that you gave yourself. Write these words down, spending as much time as you need to get them out.

Next, I want to ask you to do something that may feel unnatural or uncomfortable.

Grab a chair and sit beside it on the floor and picture the Father is sitting in the chair. Lay your head on the chair and imagine it's resting in His lap. If you don't have a chair, find a wall to lean against, close your eyes and picture the Father sitting behind you, His arms tucked around you, your head leaning back against His chest. Ask the Father to speak to those lies, those words, those names you wrote. Ask Him to speak His truth over you and then listen.

The Father delights in you,[10] you are a chosen people and God's special possession,[11] and He lavishes such rich love on you,[12] His daughter. It is because of who He calls you—because you are His daughter—that you have access to live bravely! Everything that He has, you have access to. He is courageous and you have access to courage. He is peace and you have access to peace.[13] He is love and you have access to love.[14]

Daughter, His call to you today is "take access!"

Jesus was one for bold statements. Scripture is filled with His "I AM" statements—declarations of who He is because of who the Father is (i.e., the Bread of Life, the Light of the World, the Good Shepherd.)[15] As a part of

God's family, His only Son, Jesus had access to all God has.

Today, I want you to write out your own declarations—I AM statements of truth that you can walk in because you have been given access! For example:

I am courageous.
I am known.
I am loved.
I am…

Grab a piece of paper and write them out as the Lord speaks them to you. Then, I encourage you to place them somewhere so you can be reminded of those truths.

Daughter, you have access, so take hold of it today!

Chapter 3

He Calls Me Courageous

By Kristy Mikel

As the plane finally broke through the mass of clouds we had been flying above, my eyes took in the stunning mountains of Thailand. Vibrant green stretched across the surface in every direction, evidence of the rainy season's effect on the landscape. Staring out the window, my eyes filled with tears as the wheels touched down, bouncing lightly on the pavement. It was August 2016, and my life had taken an exciting but unexpected turn. With two tightly packed suitcases in tow, I stood with shaky confidence, stepped off the plane onto the tarmac, and took in my new home.

Just one month prior, I had worked in the office of my home church in Indiana. For twelve years I had worked in youth ministry—serving high school students, coordinating small groups, and leading short-term mission trips. Though my job was sometimes stressful, I was comfortable. I had built confidence from being in the same place all those years. It was familiar to me, something I was capable of doing. Yet the Lord had been stirring and speaking, longing to take me into a new land. Much like the Israelites whom the Lord brought out of Egypt, He longed to take me to a new place, a promised land He had called me to enter—yet everything within me questioned if I could.

This calling was what my heart wanted—to live abroad and serve alongside a ministry that empowered women—but it scared me to step into it. Those days, my heart longed more than anything else for courage.

I longed to be like David taking on a giant with unwavering confidence or Joshua marching into battle against Jericho with audacious faith. These were stories that inspired me and people I longed to be like. Yet in this season of searching for courage, the Lord led me to the story of Peter sinking among the waves in Matthew 14:22-33.

Peter Walks on the Water (a paraphrase)

After feeding a hungry crowd of five thousand, Jesus sent the disciples ahead of Him in a boat to cross the lake as He sought a quiet place to pray. Later that night, He saw the disciples were still far from shore because the wind and waves were against them. Getting up from where He was, Jesus made His way down the mountain and onto the lake. In the moonlight, the disciples saw a figure walking toward them on the waves and panicked.

"It's a ghost!" they cried out.

Then came this voice, His voice: "Take courage! It is I. Don't be afraid."

Peter answered, "Lord, if it's You, tell me to come to You on the water."

"Come on then," came His reply.

So Peter got out of the boat. Slowly stepping onto the water with one foot then the other, Peter let go of the side and walked toward Jesus. He was walking on water, and Jesus was beaming at him. Then, for a moment, Peter dropped his eyes. He looked around, noticed the waves, and froze in fear. As he did, he began to sink.

The waves now pulling him under, Peter cried out for Jesus, "Lord, save me!"

And Jesus did. Extending a steady hand, He reached down and pulled Peter up. Then Jesus leaned in close and whispered to His friend, "Why did you doubt?"

For years, I read this story with a certain tone—an exasperated Jesus telling a fearful Peter to trust Him yet again. I pictured Jesus frustrated as He reached out to Peter, who sank under the waves he had been standing on top of moments before. I imagined Jesus' question to Peter filled with a certain amount of angst.

This is Jesus we're talking about. Peter had seen Him do so many incredible things! One of the first disciples Jesus called, Peter and his brother were out fishing when Jesus' call reached their ears. Immediately leaving their nets, Peter and Andrew jumped out of their boat, ran to shore, and followed Him. For three years Peter walked closely with Jesus, shadowing His every move. Wherever Jesus went, Peter followed. Visiting town after town, Peter was on His heels watching as Jesus healed the sick and raised the dead to life. When people brought the lame before Him, Peter witnessed firsthand as Jesus commanded them to their feet and their legs found new strength. Awed like the crowds who surrounded him, Peter had a front-row seat to the countless miracles of Christ. So why did he now doubt the One who called to him from across the waves?

It didn't make sense.

But then, what if I was asking the wrong question? What if the story of Jesus calling Peter out of the boat and onto the waves is not the story of a man who doubted the One who called him? What if it's instead a story of a man who doubted his own ability to come?

Sometimes Come Means Climb

Two years into life in Thailand, I felt the strain of missionary life. The season I found myself in was busy and chaotic. I missed home, my family, and my friends. Cultural stress was taking its toll. Everything in Mae Sot differed from my home in Indiana—the language, the stores, the food, the people. And my heart longed for something familiar.

I love living in Thailand. Here, the surrounding mountains call my spirit to adventure and explore. My heart comes alive with every waterfall, every rice field filled with color, every back road leading to some place new. Yet, some days are a real challenge and leave my heart aching for a chance to step away. In those moments, I reach for my headphones and pull my green bike off the rack. There's something about pedaling down the back roads of Mae Sot that refreshes my soul.

During one of these soul-refreshing moments, I cycled out of town and down an abandoned highway. A strong wind met me head on, forcing me to slow down and reminding me of how exhausted my body felt. As I turned onto a side road, I immediately confronted a steep, uphill climb. Looking at the road ahead was so discouraging. I could see it rising toward the sky, and all I could think of was how exhausted I already was. Tired and frustrated, I thought to myself, *I don't want to climb this mountain! I just want it to move!*

Shifting into my lowest gear, my legs felt the pain of trying to inch up the mountain. My mind screamed at me to get off and walk to the top, but I didn't want to face the disappointment of giving up. So I continued up the hill. My legs cramped. My side burned. My lungs ached. Tears spilled from my eyes and ran down my reddened cheeks. I was so frustrated. Desperately reaching for strength, my mind grabbed hold of the song playing through my headphones. "You taught me the courage,"[16] came the words. It was a phrase I needed for more than just the mountain in front of me. This was a season of needing courage.

Courage, Kristy. You don't want to give up. So don't! I thought to myself.

Shaking my head as if to throw off doubt, I leaned forward, took a deep breath, and slowly inched my way up the mountain. And after some struggle, the road leveled off. At the top, my eyes took in the beautifully carved mountains of Thailand and Myanmar and vibrant fields ready for harvest. I let out a deep sigh and looked over my shoulder at the climb behind me.

Tears ran down my cheeks. I had nothing left to give, but I had done it. I had climbed the mountain that felt impossible.

After riding the rest of the way home, I collapsed on the floor to catch my breath. Closing my eyes, I pictured the climb up the mountain and recalled my thoughts as I struggled to reach the top. *I don't want to climb this mountain. I just want it to move.*

Tears filled my eyes again as I thought about the season I was in. I felt so far out of my league—each day trying to learn something new, each day feeling as though I couldn't do what the Lord led me here to do. My fears felt like they might win. My insecurities overwhelmed me, and all I wanted was for the Lord to take them away.

"Kristy," came His gentle voice, "I want you to climb this mountain too."

I held my breath, unsure of how to respond. The Lord had seen my fears. He knew my doubts. I cried out to Him about them every day. Still, in this season, they threatened to overwhelm me—tempting me to give up and pick an easier way.

I was working alongside my friend as the codirector of a ministry. We did business as a café and sewing center, but I didn't know the first thing about business! All of our meetings about spreadsheets and numbers, projections and business goals were like a foreign language to me. My mind struggled to keep up and my heart felt so discouraged. How was I supposed to do this? It weighed me down, the doubts and fears that daily rose to the surface. I felt like an imposter, like the one person who didn't belong in the room. Add to that the cultural stress of being far from home and family, surrounded by languages I couldn't understand, and you had me—a total mess.

"Why?" I asked the Lord. "Why won't you just take the fears and insecurities away like I've been asking you to?" I sobbed.

Gently He spoke again, "Because I believe in your ability to overcome them."

Understanding the Call to Come

The Father has ached for His people to recognize His belief in them from the very beginning. From Moses on Mount Sinai, whom God called to lead an entire nation out of slavery, to Jesus calling each of His disciples to follow Him. How the Father has longed for us to know the sound of His voice. He has longed for us to hear what He says! Yet, if we don't know His nature, we risk misinterpreting the sound of His voice and the very words He speaks.

Remember the moment Jesus called Peter to step out of the boat?

"Come," He called from across the waves. *Come.*

Legs shaking and knuckles white, Peter stepped out into a beautiful invitation from a teacher and friend—not a demand from a frustrated Jesus.

This was the same invitation Jesus had given to Peter when He first called him to leave his net and boat behind—an invitation to come and follow Him. These same words Jesus continued to speak to Peter and the disciples as they traveled with Him from town to town, witnessing Him heal the sick, restore sight to the blind, and speak life over the dead. Jesus was always inviting His disciples to be a part of what He was doing.

"You can do what you have seen me doing, so come," was Jesus' continual message to all who followed Him.

Peter knew this voice. He recognized it. He'd spent so much time around it. He knew the nature of Jesus and understood the kinds of things He would say. And it was because Peter knew Jesus, because he knew the sound of His voice, that he stepped out onto the water.

Friends, let's not miss this moment! With a single word, Jesus was assuring Peter of this one thing: "You can do this. I'm inviting you to take courage and come!"

So Peter took a step. Filled with faith in the One who had called him to come, Peter stepped, believing he could do the very thing Jesus invited him to do. Yet a moment later, Peter dropped his eyes. The howling wind and crashing waves reminded him of where he was, and fear and doubt rose to the surface. And seeing the impossible place he was standing, Peter thought, *I can't walk on top of these waves!*

And it was in this moment I finally saw it—a powerful moment of trust lost among the waves as Peter missed the full invitation of Jesus.

Take Courage and Come

"Take courage," Jesus called out to the disciples from the waves. "Peter, take courage and then come."

This was the full invitation of Jesus. It was not just an invitation to come out onto the waves that surrounded him. This was an invitation to take hold of something that would help steady Peter's wobbly feet. And Jesus gives us the same invitation. Take courage and come.

The season I was in had plenty of questions and very few answers. Here I was in Mae Sot, Thailand—in the very place the Lord had called me to come. I had heard His invitation and seen all the ways He continued to provide. So I took a step. Yet, much like Peter, I had stepped into a place where fear and doubt continued to lurk beneath the surface, reminding me of where I was, threatening to overwhelm my mind and drown me in the rising fear.

As the Lord revealed the truth of that word "come," I understood the full invitation of Jesus. Like He did with Peter, the Father believed in my ability to overcome the very things that overwhelmed me. And, like Peter, he had invited me not only to come but to take hold of something He had given me to access.

Daughter, take courage.

Friends, fear has stopped me more times than I care to admit. It has been a daily struggle to come when I stare in the face of fear. Yet when fear gains control, I lose sight of the Father because all I can see is everything that's hard, intimidating, and seemingly unmovable. When fear gets a voice, the truth of the Father becomes harder to hear over the lies that fear speaks: *You can't. You'll fail. You're not good enough!*

My whole life, not only that one season, has carried these lies—lies that give fear a place the Father never intended it to have. And so the Father invites us to take courage because He recognizes that fear will wait in the places He's called us to and in the things He's called us to do. He understands the power of fear shaking us and redirecting our steps. The Father invites us to take hold of courage as we come because it's what we need to stand among the waves.

I don't know about you, but for me courage is sometimes so hard to hold. Faced with fear, my emotions quickly get the better of me, allowing my insecurities to take hold. The subtle whispers of the enemy sound more like deafening shouts in my ears. I can't tell you the number of moments I've sat crying over the process of even writing this book. As the Father has invited me to step into this beautiful calling with Him, the enemy constantly whispers that someone else could do this better or that my story carries no merit. There have been so many moments throughout my life where insecurity, doubt, and fear rise, seeking a seat at the table. And how willingly I give in some days. As I accept fear, insecurity, and doubt, they take a seat at the table where peace, rest, and courage were once sitting.

"Daughter, take courage," the Father calls to us. "Give courage a seat at the table instead of fear. You have access to my courage. Moment by moment, day after day, take courage and come."

This is what it means to live bravely.

An Invitation to Live Bravely

Jesus' invitation to Peter is the same one that has echoed throughout every generation from the beginning of time. This was the invitation to Moses to lead the nation of Israel out of slavery in Egypt—take courage because I am with you. It was the same invitation to Joshua, who would continue to lead God's people into the Promised Land— be strong and courageous, for I am with you wherever you go. Each of them had access to courage because the Father promised to be with them. He promised to meet them where they were going. And just as He invited Peter to walk to where He was among the waves, the Father invites us to take courage and come!

Friends, we have a Father who believes in our ability to look fear in the face and command it to move. We're about to walk where fear is standing because Jesus said we could come!

In Thailand and at Braverly, I get to walk alongside women who daily try to live this out. Every day I get to see these women take courage as they learn new things like baking, sewing, and doing business. I see their confidence grow as they step into things they've never done before. I get to do life with a community of incredible women who both challenge and encourage me. Here, we are learning to courageously follow Jesus together!

Every day is a new day of not fully knowing what's coming my way. More times than not, I question, *"How do I do that?"* Yet we are a community of women learning together to take one more courageous step forward because Jesus says we can!

Sometimes I think we look at the mountains in our life—a heartbreak, a tough family situation, a fear that feels impossible to move past—and yell at them to move because deep down, we don't believe we can climb them. We don't believe we have what it takes to push through, hold on, keep trying, or trust we'll get through it. In our shouts, tears, exhaustion, and unbelief, the Lord continues to speak His gentle invitation, "I want you to climb this mountain. Take courage and come."

It's not because He's uncaring or doesn't want to help. Our Father doesn't like to see us struggle or feel like we should give up. Yet sometimes He invites us to come because He wants us to see in ourselves what He has always seen. We need to go through the pain and struggle of the climb to realize we were always capable of reaching the top. And when we do, we need to remember this mountain won't be the last we climb.

There will always be one more hill, one more wave, one more chance to take another step. Like Peter, the waves we walk on today may lead us out into deeper waters tomorrow. But daughter, take courage because the One who invites you to risk the safety of the boat for the unknown of the waves believes in your ability to come! The Father believes in us, and because of this belief, we carry the courage to live brave.

The Pause

Sister, you are brave, and you are courageous!

The Father believes in you. What a wonderful thought! He believes you can do hard things. He believes you can look fear in the eyes and say to it, "I won't listen to you because Jesus said I can come!" The Father has given you access to courage, and He invites you each day to take courage and follow Him.

Every single day we face fears and insecurities. Each day we face moments of questioning if we can do what the Lord is asking us to do. Fear, insecurity, and doubt fight for a seat at the table—longing to cast aside peace, truth, rest, and the courage the Father promises we can have.

So pause and acknowledge fear. Let's take a moment to understand the things that hold us back. What are they? Let's give them a name. In the space below or a journal, write out some of those daily fears and insecurities that rise to hold you back.

When Jesus called Peter from across the waves, He acknowledged fear. He knew it was present, and so He spoke to fear by calling out to His disciples, "Take courage." In that moment, what the disciples needed to know was that they could access courage. They could choose it over fear.

As you look over the fears and insecurities that often rise to the surface and cause you to doubt what you're capable of, think about what Jesus says.

He calls you courageous!

So, today, we will speak to fear. We know it exists, and it wages war against us. We command fear to move because we are about to walk where it's standing. Jesus said we can come!

Write Your Charge

In every grand battle scene, there's a charge—an attempt to fill the soldiers with courage. At Braverly, our charge is to live brave, dream bravely, and influence bravery. We will daily choose courage over fear, trust over doubt, truth over lies. We believe our brave living can influence those around us to step into their own brave stories, and so we will take courage and come!

Today, I want you to write your charge—your prayer for living brave.

God's Word is one of the most powerful tools we have. We believe His Word is truth, and we know the only way to overcome fear and lies is with the truth! As you write your charge/prayer, maybe you need a reminder of some of His truth. You can take a moment to read through one or all of the Scriptures below—truth about what the Father believes about you and how He sees you! Then write your charge and place it somewhere you will see and remember.

- Deuteronomy 31:8
- Joshua 1:9
- Psalm 27:1
- Isaiah 41:10; 41:13
- 1 Corinthians 16:13
- 2 Timothy 1:7

As I wrote this chapter, the Lord spoke these words to me I want to share with you. This is my prayer for each of you. Let these words from the Father encourage your heart.

He Calls Me Courageous
Written by Kristy Mikel
I see your courage, when you see your fear
I know you're capable, when you feel unclear
I see your courage; I know your name
I call you Courageous, so walk unashamed

I see your courage, no need to look grave
Each day stepping forward, that's how you live brave
I see your courage, I'll help lead the way
Together, Beloved, we'll win this day!

I see your courage, I've called you to come
I know you're capable, though you'd rather run
I see your courage, so walk unafraid
Together, Beloved, let's dare to live brave!

Chapter 4

He Created a Place for Me

By Kate Berkey

Defined by a Lie

I think we all have those things others have said or done to us—things that come to define and scar us in ways we don't fully understand. Life moves on after the pain or trauma, and we try to forget until we can't anymore. In that moment of reckoning, everything bulldozes to the front of our hearts and minds, and we can no longer ignore the hurt.

For me, careless words said from one child to another came to define me. The words were simple, the demand clear. "You need to learn your place." My brother said this to me—the one I looked up to, the one I thought was my friend, the one I thought would protect me. He said it in a moment of anger and sibling rivalry, and even though I was only a child, his words devastated my heart. This place—the one he thought I needed to learn—was beneath him. I was beneath him because I was his little sister. I was younger, and I was a girl. That's what I heard.

All these years later, I still remember the way his demand knocked the air from my lungs and made my head spin. I remember the way I fought off tears and fierce, balled-fist anger. Even then I knew I shouldn't have to fight for my place. My place was bigger than what he thought, and my age or gender didn't diminish me. I believed in the depths of my being that this kind of demand shouldn't come from my family or someone I trusted and loved. But, especially in our religious conservative culture, my brother had the power. I had little to none. It seemed no one dreamed of giving it to little girls.

For years, I carried the weight of his words, letting them define what I was capable of. "Learn your place" haunted me and locked me in a cage built with impenetrable walls. I didn't just hear them echo in my mind. I felt them in my soul every time I dared to step into a place or role outside of what my culture said was normal or acceptable. They made me second guess and question and doubt myself, and these words broke my relationship with my brother.

It took an honest conversation dripping with vulnerability and tears until we reached reconciliation and healing. Today, my brother is one of my biggest fans, supporters, and encouragers. Often, he will send me a card or text to remind me he's proud of and believes in me. He sees me as a woman with authority and a powerful voice, and he gives me the courage to step into the places people say I shouldn't be.

But when I think of the bondage I sat in for so many years and the place I sit now, I wonder why it took me so long to have the difficult conversation in the first place. Until this conversation—until I dismantled the lies that defined my place in this world—the phrase, "learn your place," wrecked me. To make matters worse, as I grew up and experienced more of my culture and church tradition, it was as if everyone was screaming this same demand to women everywhere.

"Learn your place!" They seemed to shout.

And they limited this place to the home—cooking, cleaning, and doing laundry. While men built empires, we raised babies and changed diapers. Although this is a beautiful and high calling, I couldn't help but feel suffocated—held hostage while my heart dreamt of and longed for something different.

If my place in the Kingdom was as a silent bystander, a support to men, a good wife and mom, why did the Father give me the gift of writing and dreams to change the world through words and stories? Or what if I never even got married or had kids? My place was bigger than the home, right? Was I confined to a short list of possibilities while doors flung themselves wide open for my brothers?

Was this the Kingdom of God?

Put Down Your Sword

Friend, can we pause for a moment? Few conversations cause such division and defensiveness than those about a woman's place in this world—especially in the church.

"Uh, do you mean feminism?" People in the church ask with trembling voices, hands poised to draw their swords.

I grew up among highly religious conservative groups that defined which roles men and women could have. More times than not, tradition rather than truth determined these roles. Although I didn't belong to these religious groups, their thinking came to define the greater culture of my hometown, limiting my ideas of women's roles.

This is my history, and you have your own. Perhaps you've seen women empowered and free to live fully in their God-given gifts and abilities, whether from the home, the corner office, or the church. Or maybe you've seen women abused, taken advantage of, and disempowered in unimaginable ways. No matter where we come from, each of us has experienced the tension of women in our world and in Christendom, because whether we like it or not, Scripture isn't as black and white as we might like.

Often, we have to hold things in tension. The Lord permits something in one chapter, and in another, He seems to say "no." In our attempts to understand, we search for historical and cultural context, but no matter how much we research and learn, some things will always hold tension. We're human—limited and imperfect. We can't know everything.

I believe the role of women in the church and our world is one of those many areas of tension—of accepted and banned, of dehumanized and celebrated. Some stories in the Bible treat women as subhuman, and in others they are queens and apostles, judges and prophets, leading God's people and not because men weren't available. They led because they were qualified, gifted leaders. Because that's who the Father created them to be.

So no matter where you come from, you need to trust that this chapter isn't an attempt to elevate women and diminish men. That's not the way the Father designed His Kingdom. He created Eve to stand beside Adam and Adam beside Eve. It takes both men and women contributing their gifts as leaders and followers, visionaries and encouragers to build the Kingdom. Friends, we can learn from each other. We can empower and support each other. I believe very little stirs more joy in the Father than when He sees His people live with this kind of wholehearted unity.

Our world is full of bold, daring men and women who have and are and will continue to transform lives. These bold, daring women don't diminish men. Rather, they enhance them in the same way that men and their dreams should enhance our own. This is the Kingdom of God, and the Father longs to see you use your unique gifts, abilities, and dreams to build His Kingdom because He gave them to you. He delights in dreaming with you, His daughter, and your culture or church or community does not limit your dreams.

That's what you need to know.

So, do me a favor. No matter what you believe about women's roles, put down your sword. Go on this journey with me and trust me. You might disagree with or feel frustrated at some points. That's okay. Sit with those emotions and thoughts. Don't be afraid of the questions they stir. Talk to Jesus about them and allow Him to reveal what is true.

Sister, you have a place in the Kingdom of God, and it's bigger than you could ever imagine.

Creating a Bigger Space

My journey to discovering my place in the Kingdom was filled with books and commentaries, podcasts and sermons, anger and tears, and moments of total surrender. I've cried out to the Father more times than I can remember, totally confused about how to reconcile verses in the Bible. To be honest, I still don't know what to do with some of them, but I've found hope in Jesus' relationship with women throughout the gospels.

In these interactions, Jesus becomes more than a two-dimensional character. He reflects the Father's true heart. In these stories, I see His longing to free the oppressed and usher the marginalized into the Kingdom. And I sense the deepest kind of love—one that welcomes the people that culture had written off.

One of these stories is Jesus' interaction with Mary and Martha in Luke 10. It's a familiar story, one I've heard pastors teach many times. They've talked about the dangers of being too busy and the reasons we need to be with Jesus. I've even heard sermons about the way Jesus talked to Martha like He was an exasperated dad. In all my years of church, I'd never heard the historical and cultural context of this story until I listened to a message by Pastor Kris Vallotton.[17]

Suddenly, the question plaguing my mind became, *What if this story celebrates the countercultural place Jesus created for women rather than a warning against busyness?* What if Martha's demand didn't exasperate or frustrate Jesus? What if, more than anything, He wanted Martha to recognize her place with Him and in the Kingdom? This place was so much bigger than she knew or her culture, tradition, or religion could express.

If this was true—if Jesus was destroying cultural lies and creating unprecedented space for His beloved women—this is a truth worth celebrating, teaching, and clinging to.

The story begins with Jesus and the disciples' journey to Jerusalem. They were on a mission, but when they got to a particular village, they paused, visiting the home of Martha. Being the good hostess, Martha cooked and cleaned. She did everything her culture expected of her when a guest was in her house. And I've got to believe she didn't mind this. My guess is she was honored to have Jesus as her guest. But while she worked, her sister, Mary, sat at Jesus' feet, listening to His every word.

The peaceful scene pauses with an abrupt interruption from Martha. She storms into the room and demands, "Lord, don't you think it's unfair that my sister left me to do all the work by myself? You should tell her to get up and help me."[18] Frustrated and appalled, Martha calls out her sister's actions and blatant rebellion of the law. Not only is Mary refusing to help Martha, but she is sitting at the feet of a teacher, learning from a man.

Jesus' response is so simple and beautiful and culture shaking that it's almost easy to miss. "Martha, my beloved Martha. Why are you upset and troubled, pulled away by all these many distractions? Mary has discovered the one thing most important by choosing to sit at my feet. She is undistracted, and I won't take this privilege from her."[19]

Friends, can we pause for a moment? Jesus' words drip with the extravagant love He pours on His daughters, and I don't want to breeze past it. At His feet, Mary sat completely undistracted, and Jesus refused to take that privilege from her.

If we only see a quick lesson about avoiding busyness, about being still in Jesus' presence, we miss the space, the privilege women hold with Jesus. This is a real life, flesh and blood, culture-changing-before-your-eyes kind of story. Jesus doesn't just tell a parable about how we should treat women or their space in the Kingdom. He shows them, and He shows us.

A Place of Ownership

As Luke recounted Jesus' interaction with Mary and Martha, he would have been very aware of the crazy, countercultural things happening, and I can't help but admire his words. In his day, women, land, and homes were the property of men. Women were the helpers, the supporters of men. Men held all the power, rights, and privileges, and this meant they held ownership.

Yet, Jesus went to *Martha's* house. This is no small detail. There is no mention of Martha's father or husband or brother because this home was Martha's, and Jesus didn't cling to the traditions of His culture at the expense of ignoring truth. He looked at Martha and saw her, not those who claimed ownership over her. He saw her sister. He saw her house, and this is the space He entered.

If we believe Jesus was an intentional man, think about His subtle message and the ripples it caused. He showed love and honor simply by stepping into a place most men, especially male teachers, would have avoided. Not only would it have forced the men in the room to confront the laws preventing them from teaching women, it would have forced them to acknowledge the woman as the owner rather than the supporter.

But these women were Jesus' friends, and this house was Martha's. I believe Jesus longed to celebrate Martha, to recognize the home she owned, the space she created for her family and her guests. In a time when normative thinking considered women the property of men, Jesus stepped onto property owned by a woman. With each step, He dared to honor the space her culture and tradition believed she had no right to claim.

So, what does this mean for us today? It means we have ownership in the Kingdom. When God created all those good and beautiful things in the Garden, He created man and woman. He called the woman a helper, but the Hebrew word used here is so much more than a supporter. The word is `ezer, and of the twenty-one times it's used in Scripture, sixteen of those times describe the ways in which the Father helped Israel. It describes the way he fought for and rescued and saved them when they most needed it.

Our place of ownership is rooted in the name our Father gave us in the Garden. We are `ezers—fighters, defenders, builders, and helpers. Our place of ownership tells us we take up an invaluable space in the Kingdom. It says that tradition and religion does not define our place in the Kingdom of God. It's not controlled by culture. It's not limited by those who seem to hold power.

It means the Father looks at us and our place in the Kingdom and declares this space for `ezers—helpers, co-laborers. His Kingdom is for men, children, and the elderly, and it is for women. We hold power, privilege, and rights by being daughters in the family of God.

We have ownership.

A Place of Relationship

This place of ownership leads us into Jesus' response to Martha. It's one I can't quite shake—*my beloved Martha*. When we read this story, it can be easy to imagine Jesus shaking His head as He responds, as if we're in *The Brady Bunch*. "Martha. Martha. Martha."

But Jesus' tone wasn't that, was it? He didn't feel annoyed or frustrated or too busy to deal with the person in front of Him. Martha, my beloved Martha. This is huge—a countercultural way to talk to women. It's a tone of love and kindness. It's a place of belonging. She's not just Martha. She's His beloved Martha—not an indication of ownership but of relationship.

So often I think we view Jesus as this impersonal guy, disconnected and void of emotion, and when we give Him emotion, He can sound a little exasperated. But more and more, I am convinced Jesus addresses all of His children like this, with that beautiful name—my beloved. He certainly sent shock waves through the room when He addressed Martha as His beloved. I can almost hear the gasps when Jesus not only disregarded the law by letting Mary stay but also showed deeply tender, compassionate love toward Martha.

Friend, He calls us beloved too—His beloved. As His beloved we have access to everything because we're in the family. This word is one of kinship, of family rather than ownership and control. It's the kind spoken to daughters. The life and freedom Jesus spoke over the woman who had bled for twelve years is the same life and freedom He spoke over Mary and Martha. And it's the same message for you and me.

Jesus doesn't dismiss you. He pulls you in closely and calls you by name. More and more, the Father's voice sounds like this to me—one of kindness, gentleness, and grace. It's a voice and tone that creates space for us—all of us. We have a place of relationship with Him because of His deep love. We are not just beloved. We are His beloved.

This name pulls us in close, right beside Jesus, a place we can live, dream, and work from—a place of authority in the Kingdom because of Jesus.

On that day with Mary and Martha, Jesus, beloved Jesus, made a giant statement—I see this hardworking woman. I know her name, and I love her. She is my beloved Martha.

You have a place in the Kingdom of God, and it is a place of value. Here you are known and loved and called beloved.

A Place with Jesus

If you haven't caught it, those in the room probably weren't celebrating the space Jesus created for Mary and Martha in this interaction. There's just no way around this—it was illegal for Mary to sit at Jesus' feet. She shouldn't have been there. For hundreds of years, it was against the law to teach women. So, can you just imagine this scene unfolding?

Jesus comes into Martha's home. She greets Him and offers Him a room to teach. As she turns to prepare the food and table, she expects Mary to be right behind her. Instead, her sister follows Jesus. Everyone takes their seats, and Mary takes the one place she doesn't belong—directly in front of this teacher named Jesus. She doesn't even try to hide in the back or sneak in later. She doesn't wait for the men with higher social rank and honor to take the best seat. That seat is hers, and she unashamedly takes it. Shocking everyone, Jesus doesn't kick her out of the group or the room. He doesn't tell her she doesn't belong, that she doesn't deserve to be where she is. He doesn't scold her or make a scene. He doesn't dehumanize her or treat her the way the laws and traditions require. He creates space for her and teaches.

I can just imagine the disciples' faces. I can see their furrowed brows, almost hear them whisper to one another. When Martha finally interrupts Jesus, I hear a sigh of relief from the crowd—finally someone had the guts to say something about Mary's presence. They all thought it. Martha just said it.

But sweet Jesus' response is so very different from what everyone expected. He is the One who created room for the marginalized and oppressed. He came to overturn traditions and laws that existed to diminish His people. With every breath, He spoke truth and life to those whom others tried to forget.

"Mary has discovered the one thing most important by choosing to sit at my feet. She is undistracted, and I won't take this privilege from her."[20]

His words overflow with joy because Mary has found her rightful place. It is a privilege to sit with Jesus, and He is delighted to watch Mary embrace this privilege. He does more than create space for His beloved. He fights for this place. He dismisses those who say she should return to where she belongs. There is something much more important for Mary, and she found it. She spotted it in Jesus when He walked in the room, and she had the courage to step into her rightful place beside Him. It hadn't been accessible to her or other women for hundreds of years, but Jesus held it out with an open hand.

Mary knew all eyes were on her. She knew what she was doing, knew that she was going against deeply upheld laws, customs, traditions, and prejudices. But I have to believe Mary sensed something bigger, something deeper. Jesus was different, and she knew that. The way He treated the poor and the sick and the children—all people who were oppressed—was counter to the best of the best in her religion. She had to have wondered if women were on the list of people Jesus came to set free.

That day, Jesus did more than unlock the chains binding women. He laid a red carpet, inviting them to take their place in the Kingdom. This place is with Him, doing the things that culture, religion, and tradition say is impossible. No one recorded what Jesus taught that day because I'm not sure it mattered as much as His actions. They did more than words ever could.

Learn Your Place

All of that is incredible, but can I be honest? I've spent a lot of time feeling angry with the Father about the way women are treated in Scripture and our world. Have you read the Old Testament? More often than not, we see women treated worse than animals. For years, I couldn't reconcile these stories with the heart of the Father. I've talked to Him about the role of women. I've watched cultures and countries diminish, second guess, discredit, and devalue us, and what's worse, I've seen the same in

Christian circles. I've said, "If this is God's Kingdom, I want out." I'm tired of being told to learn my place.

And then Jesus did what He's been doing for thousands of years—slowly helping people see past lies and religion to His true heart. It wasn't like I experienced one huge moment—a lightbulb over my head. It was a slow change that began when I worked in ministry. On my team, I was one of the few women who had a different job than the other ladies I worked with, and whether they realized it or not, others often narrowly defined my role in ways my male coworkers didn't experience.

I pushed hard against the roles it seemed I was destined to fit into. I had tough conversations with my leaders and coworkers. I challenged them but also let them check my heart—knowing that we all need grace and the space to grow. Over and over again, I fought for my place at the table, like Mary taking up space close to Jesus. All of this—the direct conversations, the fighting for my place at the table—went against every fiber of my being. At my core, I am a peacemaker and peacekeeper, but I've learned that sometimes peacemaking can look like fighting battles. Sometimes it looks like charging into conflict to find true peace.

In the early days, I second-guessed myself often, asking why I was doing what I was doing. I fought off that old phrase "learn your place" and wondered what gave me the right to fight against the space others tried to fit me into. In my heart, I desperately wanted to believe the Father didn't limit my place in His Kingdom to what tradition said. And more than anything, I longed to take the place Jesus created for me, using my gifts to build His Kingdom rather than slip into what others expected of me.

For years, I waded through the messy, challenging work of letting Jesus define my place in the Kingdom of God—both inside and outside of my 9-5 role. In this season, the Father spoke new life to the gifts He's given me, showing me the authority I have and the power of my voice and ideas. He showed me warriors from Scripture like Deborah, Esther, and Rahab—women who shook cultures and changed the course of history in their own way.

I tried to follow their example. I learned to speak up, value my voice, and hope others would do the same. And in so many ways, I'm still on this journey—this unlearning and relearning my place. But I can say with confidence that my place is with Jesus, at His feet, learning from Him, being with Him. It's walking with Him, doing what I see Him doing. I own my place in the Kingdom when I teach and love others, lead and prophesy, overturn tradition for tradition's sake, and break the spirit of religion. He calls me Kate, His beloved Kate, and my place is with Him, using the gifts He's given me to build His Kingdom.

And this is your place too. It's our place. Some of us lead Bible studies or nourish neighbors and families with delicious food. Some build the Kingdom by building families and raising babies. Others are leaders of organizations, pastors, seamstresses, baristas, or soldiers, and isn't this beautiful?

Jesus looks at us and declares, "Daughter, my beloved daughter, join me in the Kingdom. Teach and preach. Lead and let others lead you. Nourish your community. Fight for your country. Disciple others. Build businesses. Create homes of hospitality. Bring your gifts to the table and take your place."

As we find the space Jesus creates for us, we will run into obstacles, challenges, and people who believe we do not belong. This battle to define women's place in the Kingdom of God has been going on since the garden, but we need to cling to truth.

The Father calls us beloved, and this profound name invites us into a relational space with Jesus filled with the deepest love, kindness, and power. Jesus creates space for us right beside Him. He invites us, encourages us, and delights in us when we join Him. And He gives us ownership simply through the name given to us in Eden. We are `ezers—helpers, fighters, defenders, and co-laborers in this beautiful task of building the Kingdom of God.

All of these truths give us the permission and calling to dream bravely. There are women who believe their gender defines their dreams and limits their role in the Kingdom. But in Jesus, we see something different. Sister, `ezer, beloved woman, Jesus creates a place for you so much bigger than you could imagine.

So take your place and dream with the Father.

The Pause

Let's sit with the words the Father calls us. Grab a pen or pencil and write down these names:

Daughter

Beloved

`Ezer

These are names of privilege, relationship, and authority. They remind us that we have ownership in the Kingdom of God and a place beside Jesus because we are in His family. As you think about your place in the Kingdom, what does it look like?

Do you feel limited to step into this place? If so, how do you feel limited? Take a minute to write out your thoughts and answers to these questions in the space below or your journal.

Whether you feel limited or not, the truth still remains—we have a place of ownership, we have a place of relationship, and we have a place with Jesus. Which of these truths do you need to claim the most and why does that truth speak so deeply to you? What lie, fear, or insecurity does it speak to? Write out your thoughts.

Beloved daughter, we need to remember that we have a place of authority in the Kingdom of God. Write out a prayer that declares your place with the Father. Don't be afraid of it sounding too powerful or too full of authority. Remember, we have access to everything as daughters. Root this prayer in truth—a place of ownership, relationship, and abiding with Jesus.

Once you have written it, I want you to do something bold. I want you to write out the prayer—part or all of it—and post it in the place that feels most limiting to you. For me, this is my desk. For you, this place might be on your mirror, at work, in the kitchen, or on your dresser. Post it somewhere you see often to remind you of the place the Father creates for you in the Kingdom.

Then let's embrace the freedom that comes when we learn our place with the Father, and let's begin to dream with Him.

Chapter 5

He Calls Us to Surrender

By Kristy Mikel

Are we really going to spend an entire chapter on surrender?

It's a word that makes us uncomfortable, right? I don't feel like anybody enjoys talking about surrender, about giving up or laying down something we've longed to hold. We've just celebrated how the Father creates a space for us to dream with Him, and now we're supposed to surrender? Yes, but before you close this book in disappointment or frustration, I invite you to come on this uncomfortable journey with me and discover something you might not expect to find.

A Word of Promise

Heading into my freshman year of college, I hadn't declared a major and didn't know what I would do with my life. There was so much pressure to know which career path to lock into for the next four years, and as a floundering 18-year-old, I felt ill-equipped to make such big life decisions. But college naturally followed high school, so to college I went. I didn't have experience in anything, and I had no idea what the Lord was saying about my future. This is the place the Lord met me when my college hosted a week-long, global-focused Christian conference to kick off the second semester.

Each day, we gathered in the chapel to hear from a guest speaker. And I'll be honest with you, I have no idea what he spoke about. I don't remember a single message. But what I do remember is how the Lord completely changed the course of my life in a matter of ten very confusing minutes.

The speaker ended the last service with an invitation, and without hesitation students flocked to the front ready to commit to whatever he had challenged them toward. Meanwhile, I sat God-struck, for lack of a better word, in my seat with tears streaming down my face. I honestly didn't know what was happening. All I knew was that I needed to leave, so I grabbed my bag and made a break for the exit.

Stepping into the fresh air, I had no more clarity about what to do than I had in that stuffy chapel. I was sobbing with no idea why, so I rushed back to my dorm, grabbed my phone, and dialed a familiar number. I held the phone tight to my ear, waiting for an answer.

"Hi Sweetie," came my mom's voice.

"Mom," I got out between sobs. "I think God is calling me to Africa!"

Perhaps you're now just as confused as I was at that moment. I had no idea why I said what I said! I certainly wasn't planning on it, but when I heard my mom's voice, those are the words that poured out.

Africa—a place I had never been before, never thought about going, and knew very little about. Why on earth would I think God was calling me there? Up to that point, I had traveled overseas only one time. It was an eleven-day trip with my youth group to the mountain villages of Peru where we sang worship songs with motions and taught Bible stories to kids. And now, here I was sobbing on the phone telling my mom God was calling me to Africa. It didn't make sense, but without missing a beat, my mom encouraged me to pray about it and so began my crazy future.

It's a long story of what happened next, filled with moments of seeing God do impossible things. That summer, I boarded a plane with seventeen strangers from across America as we made our way to Kenya. It was a crazy month of ministry that brought me face-to-face with passions I never knew I had, and at the end, the Lord spoke.

"Kristy, I am calling you to the nations."

This would be the start of something incredible, I was sure of it! The Lord planted a dream in my heart and a longing for the nations, and I couldn't wait to dive in! Graduating from college three years later with an International Studies degree in hand, I was ready to go. Instead, I began working full time at my home church among the cornfields in northern Indiana.

One year passed by, then two, five, eight. I was in, ready to go, luggage bought—yet each day was filled with jobs like entering church attendance on the computer, stuffing hundreds of envelopes for mailings, and answering phones. Where was God's promise of the nations? And how long was I meant to carry it?

After ten long years of waiting, God opened the door for me to return to Kenya. I committed to serve with an organization that ran a home taking care of abandoned babies. I also dove in with the local church to do other ministry within the community. My commitment was for just one year, yet I packed my bags ready to dive in for as long as the Lord wanted me there. But as that year neared the end, the Lord made it clear it was time to go back to Indiana. Again, it didn't make sense. I thought this was the promise—I was called to the nations! Why on earth was God sending me back home?

In my desperate cries to God for answers, He led me to the story and life of Abraham in Genesis 12-21.

Abraham, the Promise Carrier

Most of us are familiar with Abraham's story. Many of us grew up singing "Father Abraham" as kids, flailing our arms and legs around as we spun ourselves into a dizzy mess. Abraham is a hallmark figure of faith. His legacy is nations! This is a man who lived out his days in the Old Testament times, yet his faith and legacy are talked about in the New Testament days of the disciples. Abraham's life deeply affected the faith of the nations for every generation that followed his own, and we can't talk about dreaming bravely without diving headfirst into his story.

This man was seventy-five years old when God called him. Seventy-five and living in his father's house, married but without children. He and Sarah longed so desperately to be parents, yet it seemed impossible for them. And then the Lord came and made this incredible promise—not only was Abraham going to be a father, but his children would be too many to count!

I can only imagine the excitement and questions that welled up within him. Without hesitating, Abraham and his wife packed all they had and left for the land God called them to. Eager to step into the promise, fully ready to go, they set out on this journey with the Lord. And yet if we look at the story, Abraham is one hundred years old by the time his son Isaac is born—twenty-five years later.

Can't you just feel the agony of that wait? God came and made this unbelievable promise that Abraham thought he would step into right away; yet one year, two years, ten years, and then twenty passed and still he was waiting. So what was Abraham doing for those twenty-five years in between?

It would be easy to read those nine chapters between the time Abraham received the promise of the Lord until the moment Isaac was born and not fully understand what they must have looked like. A lot of life happened throughout those years—a lot of questioning, a lot of doubting, and a lot of crying. How many times was Abraham tempted to think: "Did I hear you right God? Am I doing something wrong? Where is the promise of nations? I'm not getting any younger!"

Yet Abraham continued to walk in communion with God, committed to carry the promise he'd received until the day of completion. Abraham carried the promise for twenty-five long years before he held his son Isaac in his arms!

A few years back, I listened to a message by Heidi Baker—a missionary and founder and CEO of Iris Global, a worldwide mission organization with over thirty-five locations in about twenty nations. A statement she made in her message challenged my heart and burned itself into my memory forever. She shared about how the Lord has given us promises to carry, and He is looking for those who will carry His promises to full term.[21]

When I think about the life of Abraham, I bet he had no idea it would be twenty-five years from the time God promised him offspring and nations to the time he held his son. Twenty-five years of carrying a promise from the Lord, just to get to the very beginning stages of seeing it come to life. Yet faithfully he carried the promise, year after year. He wasn't just someone who received a promise from the Lord, but he took on his responsibility to carry that promise faithfully until completion.

The Bible is filled with promise carriers, people who received a word from the Lord and then carried that word until they saw it fulfilled. Hebrews 11 is full of heroes of faith who carried the promises God gave them. Mary, the mother of Jesus, was visited by the angel of the Lord who told her she was chosen to carry God's son—the One who would save the world. She was a young, virgin girl who was entrusted with this incredible promise, yet it would mean physically carrying that promise to full term—nine months of pregnancy before she gave birth to a son. Nine months of enduring obstacles, questions, and plenty of physical discomfort. Carrying the promises of God is no easy task!

Almost more remarkable than what Abraham's promise was is *how* he carried the promise. Each time the Lord spoke, reminding him of the promise he carried, Abraham built an altar. The land was littered with them— each one marking a specific moment with the Father. Abraham built altars again and again, filling the land with physical reminders that the Lord was with him and had spoken to him.

All throughout the Old Testament we encounter altars. Pieced together out of earth and stone, they were erected as tables for sacrifice—a symbol of surrender. On the altar, people slaughtered lambs, goats, or calves as offerings to the Lord—a sacrifice to cover their sin, an act of surrendering themselves before God. Before Jesus ever walked the earth and later became the once and for all sacrifice for mankind, altars were a way for people to commune with God. And so Abraham built altars all throughout the land.

"I will make your offspring great," the Lord promised.
So Abraham built an altar.
"I will make nations of you," the Lord reminded.
Another altar.

Each time his heart questioned, each time his faith wavered, Abraham returned to the altar remembering what the Lord had promised him.

Come to the Altar

It's the continual cry of God's heart for us—*come to the altar, walk with Me.*

When God led me back to Indiana after my year in Africa, I didn't understand it. I longed to see His promise fulfilled in my life. I thought I had been living in the promise! I spent the next four years trying to get back to Kenya when the Lord slammed that door in my face. All of my plans had fallen through, and I was a broken mess.

"Kristy, walk faithfully before Me," came the Lord's gentle voice. "I gave you the promise to carry, not to hold too tightly."

Do you ever feel like the Lord says things that are hard to understand? The Bible is full of these kinds of stories. Look at the Gospels. Jesus was constantly teaching through different parables—each one holding deep truth if you had ears to hear and eyes to see it.

One such parable the Lord led me to was a passage in Luke 14 where Jesus teaches the crowds following Him about the cost of being His disciple. Turning to the large crowd behind Him, Jesus spoke:

When you follow Me as my disciple, you must put aside your father, your mother, your wife, your sisters, your brothers; it will even seem as though you hate your own life. This is the price you'll pay to be considered one of My followers. Anyone who comes to Me must be willing to share My cross and experience it as his own, or he cannot be considered to be My disciple. So don't follow Me without considering what it will cost you."

Luke 14:26-28a, TPT

Bold statements and a steep cost—this was the consistent call of Jesus, one that demanded people to lay down everything they had if they followed Him. Consider Jesus' call to each of the twelve disciples, men who dedicated their entire lives to follow Him. Peter and Andrew left their nets and careers as fishermen—their very livelihood. Matthew, a tax collector, left his booth and fortune. And James and his brother John, left their nets, boat, and their father who was sitting with them when Jesus' call reached their ears! The invitation was always the same, "Come, follow Me. Lay everything else down and put Me first." This was the cost of following Jesus. This was the price of stepping into His promise.

Throughout the entire Bible, His call has remained the same. What it was for the disciples in the New Testament is no different than it was for Abraham in the Old. And it was no different than what the Lord was asking of me. *Carry the promise, don't clutch it.*

Perhaps it was time to lay it on the altar. From the moment the Lord gave me the dream, I gripped it in my hands, anticipating the day I would see it come true. I put all my hope in this promise I carried, but where was my trust in the One who had given it? I positioned myself for Kenya to be my answer. I wasn't ready to hear a "no" or "wait" or "not now" or "there's something else." What I wanted most was the promise I carried.

But much like Abraham in Genesis 22, God was calling me to the altar to meet with Him again.

Returning to his story, after twenty-five years of waiting, the promise of Isaac finally came. This would be the start of seeing God's promise fulfilled. The Lord had promised nations and offspring too many to count! Isaac was only the beginning. So it's hard to fathom what God did next.

The Story of Isaac

Year after painful year, Abraham held to the promise of God. Never forgetting the words He had spoken. Never giving up on seeing the promise fulfilled, Abraham walked faithfully with God waiting for the day, the hour, the moment the answer would come. And now thirty-six years later, God asked him to lay it on the altar. It didn't make sense. Abraham was faithful to carry the promise and now watching Isaac grow up before his eyes, the Lord wanted him to sacrifice his son—the person through whom God's promise would be fulfilled.

I'm just saying, if I was Abraham, I'd have a few questions. Yet Abraham's response amazes me. The Scripture says that early the next morning Abraham got up, got ready, and set out on the journey the Lord called him to take. There's no record of hesitation, no questions he stopped to ask—just immediate obedience to what the Lord asked him to do. How much his heart must have ached. Did tears fill his eyes as he cut the firewood, gathered the oil, and packed the knife? These were tools to sacrifice his son, God's promise. How heavy must those burdens have been to carry as he loaded them onto the donkey?

Still, Abraham and Isaac set out on the journey with two of their servants until they reached the spot where Abraham saw the mountain approaching. "Stay here," he told them, "Isaac and I will worship and then come back to you."

Um, what? Maybe Abraham wasn't thinking clearly. God said that he was to sacrifice his son, so why would he tell the servants, "we'll be right back"? Step after painful step, Abraham continued the journey. Lifting the bundle of wood from the donkey, Abraham placed it on Isaac's shoulders. I imagine Isaac gave him a questioning look and spoke up, "Hey Dad, we have the wood and oil but where is the lamb for the sacrifice?"

I can only imagine how Abraham's insides must have twisted and turned at that question. Yet without missing a beat, Abraham replied, "The Lord himself will provide it." And they continued on their journey together.

When they came to the top of the mountain, Abraham once again built an altar to the Lord. Gathering up stone after stone, he stacked them, filling the holes with mud and dirt. Did tears blur his eyes as he arranged each stone?

Did he silently choke back sobs so Isaac wouldn't hear? His only son was about to become the sacrifice on the altar.

I believe that in the midst of the process, Abraham continually chose courage. He leaned hard on his faith in the Lord and never wavered.

Arranging the wood on the altar, Abraham bound his son, lifted him up and laid him on the altar. With one hand pressed firmly against his son, Abraham lifted the knife, ready to slay him—never crying out to God for another option. Abraham's obedience was unwavering, his faith in God's promise driving him to lift that knife above his head.

God had promised him nations, a promise He would fulfill through Isaac. So if God wanted Abraham to sacrifice his son, Abraham had faith God would raise him from the dead! Abraham trusted deeply in the promise of God—his courage unmovable. After all those years of waiting, following, and being with God, he understood God's Word was true and what He promises, He will do! He had seen God do it before, giving this century-old man a son! Surely God could fulfill His promise any way He wanted to—Abraham believed it wholeheartedly.

And it was there at the altar—a place that was a symbol of surrender and sacrifice—Abraham worshiped the Lord!

When the Altar Becomes a Table

For Abraham, the altar where he laid his son became a table where the Lord provided. Abraham believed fully in this truth: *The Lord has called me to the altar, but I know this altar is a table where the Lord will provide.*

Just like he had been doing his entire life, Abraham turned this altar of sacrifice into a table of praise—remembering and trusting in the promise of the Lord! It was here he turned his gaze toward heaven, here he thanked the Father for what he had not yet received. Abraham lived a life of communion with God, returning to the table again and again to praise His name. He learned the importance of daily walking with and trusting in God—remaining faithful to the One who gave Him a promise to carry. Abraham's continual faith and obedience led him to the place where God would change the course of history. Through Abraham, all nations would be blessed. This was God's promise!

I needed to encounter Abraham's story of faith and obedience. I needed to see the story of a man who walked faithfully with God each day, who lived in His very presence. Over those years of waiting for the Lord to fulfill His promise in my life, I wrestled daily with giving Him my full attention and seeking Him above anything else. There were days I loved the promise more than the One who had given it to me. Instead, I needed to come face to face with what a life of obedience and faithfulness would cost me. Like Abraham, the Father gave me a promise to carry, and His desire was for me to walk in daily communion with Him trusting in His Word. He longed for me to surrender the very thing He'd promised, putting my trust in Him and not in the promise I carried.

Learning to live daily in the presence of the Lord would carry a far greater impact than simply moving to a place my heart longed to go. And those years spent surrounded by the cornfields of Indiana were as much about cultivating a daily relationship with the Lord as they were about growing my heart for the nations. They were years that challenged me to stay faithful in the little things like entering church attendance and setting up classrooms for small groups to meet. They were filled with conversations and people who challenged my faith by the questions they asked, and years that helped me listen and learn what the Father's voice sounds like. Through every moment, every day, every experience, God raised up in me a passion for seeing people loved, valued, known, and cared for—in whatever places He led me to and with whomever crossed my path.

This is what it looks like to dream bravely—it requires that we take those dreams the Lord gives us and give them right back to Him. Because in our hands what may look like one thing, God intends to use for another.

As I write this, I'm not in Kenya like I dreamed I would be. Instead, I live in a small town along the border of Thailand and Myanmar, doing things I never imagined I would. In my hands, God's promise looked like life in Kenya, but His promise has always been bigger than that. Daily His call to us remains the same: "Follow me, put everything else down, seek Me first."

I'm living and walking in a nation that is not my own, an unexpected answer to the Lord's promise of nations in my life. Yet I know there is more of the promise to be revealed! The Lord's not finished yet, and so daily I return to the altar laying the promise down and asking Him to do with it what He wants. As the altar becomes a table, our sacrifice becomes an offering of praise to God thanking Him for the promise we know we'll receive!

Abraham praised the Lord for the promise he carried even at the point where he laid it on the altar table, uncertain of how the Lord would fulfill it. He praised the Lord for the answer he'd not yet received, filled with faith and courage that the answer would come. It was courage that led Abraham back to the altar, courage that brought him to a place of surrender, and courage that turned that altar of sacrifice into a table of praise.

The Pause

Dreaming bravely with the Father is all about surrender. It's stepping into a place of communion with Him and laying ourselves and all that we have down on the altar crying out, "Whatever You want to do and however You want to do it, I trust You!" It's about faithfully carrying the promises and passions He gives us by giving them right back to Him, allowing Him to do with them more than we could imagine.

So today, I want to ask you to do two different things. First, take a minute to focus on surrender. Take this book or a journal and get alone with the Lord somewhere you won't be distracted. With pen and paper in hand, I want you to think about and answer the following question. This time is for you to have some honest and vulnerable conversation with the Lord, so don't be afraid to dive in.

What is a passion or dream the Lord has given you to carry? Write it down. If there's more than one, list out as many as you have.

Now, looking over your list, ask yourself this: Have I surrendered this/these things to the Lord? And if not, why?

Surrender is a scary word and an intimidating step to take. Often we fear surrender because we don't know what will happen if we give something up. Will I ever get it back? And when?

Surrender puts us in a place where we have to depend fully on someone else, but friends, can I tell you, our God is faithful! Abraham knew it and lived a life of incredible impact because of it! Abraham was not driven by fear but by incredible courage and faith in who the Father is and what He can accomplish!

Growing up, my youth pastor had a phrase he said over and over again, "A surrendered life is an empowered life, and an empowered life expects the miraculous!" When we surrender ourselves, our dreams, and our passions to God, we find ourselves in a position of needing Him to see the thing accomplished. And there is no more of an empowering position to be in than to depend on the power and strength of God in us and through us to accomplish His promises!

So beyond just answering some questions, let's take some time to write out a prayer of surrender and trust. Use the next few minutes to write openly and honestly to the Lord about the things you want to surrender. Write your own declaration of "Whatever You want, and however You want to do it, I'm in!"

The second thing I encourage you to do may be a little different from anything you've done before.

As we already discovered, Abraham littered the land God called him to with altars. These altars became reminders of what the Lord promised—monuments built out of deep trust in the Father's words. Years ago, God challenged me to build an altar—not a huge monument in my yard but a few simple stones that I placed on the dresser in my room as a reminder of God's faithfulness. On each stone, I wrote words, phrases, or specific dates of things I had seen the Lord do—moments where I experienced His faithfulness. Like the day I gave my life to Christ or received God's promise that I was called to the nations.

These stones and this altar have been a place I've returned to time and time again, recounting the promises of the Lord and His faithfulness in my life. What He says, we can count on, and what He promises, He will do!

I challenge you today to do the same. Following the example of Father Abraham, take this time to build an altar to the Lord.

Maybe you want to grab some actual stones and write on them with markers, then piece those stones together into an altar you will see and be reminded of the Lord's faithfulness. Or maybe you'd rather draw an altar in the space below or in your journal and write a prayer of praise to the Lord thanking God for the ways He's been faithful to you and praising Him for the fulfillment of His promises you have yet to receive.

Whichever you do, take a few minutes to sit in the presence of the Lord and be reminded of His goodness and faithfulness.

For Yahweh is always good and ready to receive you. He's so loving that it will amaze you—so kind that it will astound you! And he is famous for his faithfulness toward all. Everyone knows our God can be trusted, for he keeps his promises to every generation! Psalm 100:5, TPT

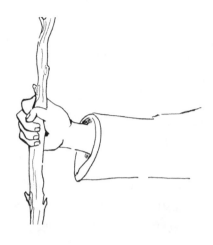

Chapter 6

He Asks Us, "What's that in Your Hand?"

By Kate Berkey

The Girl in the Crib

The woman in white pushed the door open, and my stomach dropped—like the way it does before careening down a hill on a roller coaster. My hand shook slightly as I lifted it to brush a piece of hair out of my eyes. My feet glued to the floor, only the soft touch of my mom's hand on my back urged me forward. Were my nerves as obvious to everyone else as they were to me?

It was late in the morning, and I'd lost track of the rooms we'd stepped into during the tour. They all looked similar—white walls, wooden cribs—but each held a story somehow more heartbreaking than the last. I was told this was normal for nearly every Romanian orphanage following the authoritarian rule before the 1990s. Even in 2007, the country hadn't fully recovered, and kids like these in government-run institutions were the forgotten ones.

Willing my feet forward, I followed the woman to another wooden crib pushed against another white wall. Standing beside her, I forced my eyes to focus on the girl staring back at us from inside the barred walls. Her short, curly mop of brown hair lay disheveled from lying on her back all day. She bent her knees even though her small body fit just fine in the crib. Her big brown eyes gazed up at us, wandering from the woman, to me, to my mom beside me.

The woman—one of two Christian workers in the orphanage—spoke, but I heard none of it. The girl in the crib had completely captivated all of me. The woman reached down as she talked, stroking the girl's hand. At her touch, those big, brown eyes narrowed, and a toothy grin spread across her face.

A touch—that's all it took. A hand on her own was enough to remind this beautiful girl that someone noticed her. Someone still cared for her. We remembered her. We saw her.

Her smile held our attention and wouldn't let go. The woman's voice changed from tour guide to nurturing mother. It was as if my mom and I disappeared while this sweet woman spoke in Romanian to the girl. A broken, dry laugh—the kind that comes from not speaking for a long time—came from the girl in the crib. And I heard one escape my own lips as I stood entranced by the scene unfolding before my eyes.

The woman turned to us and told us this girl's story. She had a few mental and physical handicaps, yet she brought nothing but joy to the orphanage. Because of her condition, though, it was unlikely that a family would adopt her. She would eventually age out of the system and move to another facility.

Turning back to the girl, she said, "But she's only thirteen, so she will stay with us for another five years."

My breath caught in my throat. The blood drained from my head, and through blurred vision, I watched the director reach into the crib and pull the sweet girl to her feet. We stood at eye level, this miracle and I. I raced to catch my tears before they escaped down my cheeks. She didn't need my tears. She'd given me a smile, and I wanted to give the same back to her.

The woman slid one of the girl's hands into mine, and I swallowed hard. The room spun. A high-pitched noise rang in my ears. And as my 14-year-old American-self helped this 13-year-old orphan stand in her crib, I felt a piece of me break. Whether it was my heart or my soul, I didn't know. Maybe it was a little of both.

If ever there was a moment when time stood still, it was that afternoon in the orphanage. Clocks seemed to stop as we stood together—two kids trying to make sense of their world. Eventually, though, the second hand clicked on, and the woman laid the little girl back down—her grin still spread wide across her face. Through tears, I stroked her hand, willing every part of myself to remember every detail of her face, her smile, her short curly hair, and her big brown eyes. She wasn't just a girl stuck in a Romanian orphanage. She was that full smile that made her eyes squint. She was the wonder in her face when someone walked into her room. She was the laughter when someone helped her to her feet. She was thirteen years of joy and delight, and she became a tangible representation of the question that has lingered in my heart since we stood eye to eye—two kids only one year apart carrying vastly different histories and futures.

God, what am I supposed to do?

Our Dreams Start with a Question

At only fourteen years old, this orphanage in a small Romanian town broke me in the best way. On that trip, I stared oppression and marginalization in the eye and came face to face with my privilege. This sweet girl—and a handful of other kids—left me with more questions than answers, more anger and sadness than hope and joy. Before I met them, I had asked the Father to break my heart for what breaks His, and these encounters left me breathless in a reality I couldn't ignore.

This is how so many Kingdom-building dreams start. The Father plants seeds in our lives—experiences of injustice, pain, or suffering in our world. They leave us crying out, "It's not supposed to be this way." And whether we realize it or not, these words join the echo that began in the Garden—when Adam and Eve chose their way over the Father's.

In the beginning, the Father did not create life to be full of pain and suffering, tears and toil. The Father watches this world and says, "It wasn't supposed to be this way."

But He doesn't leave us in hopelessness, wondering when or if things will change. He is the God who sees, knows, and hears, and He says, "Let's build a better way. Let's build the Kingdom."

The Kingdom of God is the very beat of the Father's heart and the motive behind His every move. It's both tangible and intangible, physical and invisible. It's the family of God—billions of image bearers who have trusted Jesus and accepted the life, love, and grace He gives. We are every nation, tribe, and language.

The Kingdom isn't far away. We are part of it today, and it changes everything. When Jesus taught us to pray, He prayed for the Kingdom to come on earth as it is in heaven. He looks at us—imperfect humans—and calls us Kingdom builders. Building the Kingdom of God isn't about building our own stories of greatness. It's about fighting for the heart of humanity to know and experience God—His love, grace, forgiveness, and life.

So when we talk about the Kingdom, this is what we're talking about—a family led by Father God. To build the Kingdom is to come to the table with our talents and kingdom size dreams and spread the name and fame of Jesus in the world.

These dreams aren't always grand or heroic. Sometimes they are, but just as often, they come in humble packages—like the Messiah born in a stable or a shepherd who became a king. So often, Kingdom-sized dreams begin with that question—"What am I supposed to do?" When we struggle and wrestle to find an answer, the Father surprises us with His response.

He leans in close and asks, "What's that in your hand?"

What's that in Your Hand?

It's a question the Lord first asked Moses in Exodus 4, and it's a question He's been asking His people ever since. After 400 years of chains, slavery had reduced Israel's hearts to mourning—their backs broken from intense manual labor. The Lord heard their cry. He saw their oppression. He knew their suffering. It wasn't supposed to be this way, but without Him, they couldn't fix anything. They couldn't reach freedom without the Father.

So the Lord looked at Moses and chose him. From the very beginning, the Father set him apart. When the Egyptians killed all the Hebrew baby boys, He saved Moses. The Father rescued him from slavery and placed him in the palace—the adopted son of the princess. Living under the privilege and rights of royalty, Moses watched his Hebrew people suffer unspeakable horrors until he couldn't any longer. In a moment of anger, he killed an Egyptian who beat a Hebrew. Afraid of what Pharaoh would do to him, Moses fled and lived as a shepherd in the wilderness for forty years.

But he didn't just run from Pharaoh. He ran from the pain he could not take away, the suffering he could not heal, the problems he could not fix. Moses tried to outrun the question, "What am I supposed to do?" But he couldn't escape the Lord. From a burning bush, the Father called to him, beckoning him onto holy ground. The Lord laid out His plan to free the Israelites and invited Moses to be a part of the greatest rescue operation the world had ever known. But with every word, Moses protested.

"Who am I to lead Israel out of Egypt? They won't listen to me. How will they know you sent me? Why would they believe me? They won't trust me. Can't you send someone else?"

I wish I could say that I would have reacted differently than him, but I'm not sure I would have. And I don't think I'm alone. All of us have probably felt overwhelmed by something the Father is asking us to do or say. Our minds run faster than we can keep up, and we fight back. We doubt Him, letting insecurities have a seat at the table. We let fear drive our hearts and the conversation.

As Moses hid behind his many questions and excuses, the Lord responded with His own question. "What's that in your hand?" He asked.

Moses looked at the object gripped by his calloused fingers and saw his staff. It was totally ordinary—worn and weathered by years of use. It was simple in every way, but in the Father's presence, nothing is simple. In the

Father's presence, the dirt beneath our feet becomes holy, and a staff becomes sacred.

The Lord told Moses to throw his staff on the ground, and Moses listened, asking no questions. Together, they watched the wood shift and shake. Moses jumped back as it morphed and took a new shape—a snake.

"Reach out and grab its tail," the Lord said.

Heart pounding, sweat pouring from his body, Moses crouched low to the ground and summoned all of his courage. The instant his fingers grasped the snake's tail, it transformed back into the object Moses had carried for years—that simple shepherd's staff.

This was the sign the Father told Him to use when he talked to the Israelites. But it was only just the beginning. Moses's staff would do more than transform into a snake. The Lord would use it as a vessel to bring freedom to a generation that knew only captivity. Through it, the Nile River turned to blood, and frogs, gnats, hail, locust, and darkness overtook Egypt. When Moses held it in the air, the Red Sea parted, and when he struck it against a rock, water gushed out. Even in war, the Lord used it to bring Israel's victory when they faced an enemy stronger and more powerful than they were.

With this one question, the Father showed all of us another way—a way of building the Kingdom using the very things we overlook. He turned simple into sacred and invited us to see the power of the ordinary.

The Simple Becomes Sacred

There's nothing special about a shepherd's staff. It was as common as phones are to us today. Moses would have carried it with him every day, almost everywhere he went. As a sheepherder, he used it to direct the sheep, corral them, and lead them home. As an 80-year-old man, it would have supported him—literally something to hold him up.

Worn from years of use, I imagine dirt and grime caked his staff. Maybe Moses's hand marked it, his fingers leaving an impression on the wood. It was an object fit for the field, not the palace. But when the Father saw it, He saw a branch from a tree He had created long ago. He saw a piece of wood His very words had formed. He created the seed that became the tree, that became the staff. It was a gift from Him, and in this gift, He saw a connection between heaven and earth.

The Father looks at us and sees the same. He created us in His image and likeness. Inside our DNA are the God-given traits we can trace back to our Father. Our personality, our talents, our desires—He created them all and said they are good. Where we see ordinary, He sees extraordinary. Where we see simple, He sees sacred. Where we see insignificance, He sees the gifts He's given us. Where we see insecurity and all the reasons something might fail, He sees a connection to the divine.

For years Moses overlooked his staff. It was just an object until he threw it at the Father's feet. And I think you and I are more similar to Moses than we would like to admit. We carry things that seem insignificant. We overlook them waiting to discover something fit for the palace when the Father has already given us holy, sacred gifts fit for the Kingdom.

As our world searches for people who will right what has been wronged, the Father asks us, "What's that in your hand?" More than anything, I believe He is looking for people who are ready to answer that question. He's looking for people to recognize the gifts He gave us when He formed us in our mothers' wombs. He aches for us to find just enough courage to see what's in our hands and throw it at His feet. Once we do, the ordinary becomes extraordinary, and the Kingdom comes a little closer.

Sacred Running Shoes

I've never thought of myself as someone with special gifts or talents. I'm as average as they come. I mean, I'm an introverted writer who prefers movies over board games, a quiet night at home to a night on the town. When the Father first asked me, "What's that in your hand," I had no response. At the time, my heart and mind felt stuck on the faces and stories and questions I first encountered in that Romanian orphanage.

Was anyone fighting for these kids? Was anyone loving them? Did anyone stroke their hands or brush their hair? Did they feel forgotten or invisible? Were they lying in their cribs all day, or did someone pull them to their feet? Did anyone snuggle them or wipe their tears or sing to them? My heart ached for the girl in the crib and the many other boys and girls who weren't receiving the love, care, and families they deserved. I couldn't see past the weight of it all to notice what the Father had put in my hand.

Unable to remain blind to the brokenness, I remember thinking, *Can anything change or will these kids stay stuck in this degrading, monotonous existence forever?* I laid awake at night, wondering about their futures. Tears ran down my cheeks as I felt compassion for them, as I suffered with them. I felt the longing of their hearts—longing for family and belonging. Certain smells took me back to that boxy building—a strange mix of rotten milk, soiled diapers, and baby powder. None of my questions had answers, and every day the aching of my heart grew stronger and louder. It was more than a feeling. It had faces, names, and stories I couldn't forget.

My prayers echoed, "What am I supposed to do with this?"

And the Father—like He does so often—leaned in and asked that simple, sacred question, "What's that in your hand?"

I had no response.

So I did what I often do when I can't figure out a problem: I ran. I'm one of those people—a runner. Running, for me, is about more than staying healthy. More times than not, it's a kind of release. It's a way to clear my mind. It's a challenge—mile after mile pushing me to keep going. But at the end of the day, running is this totally ordinary thing I do.

That day as I tied my running shoes, the Father asked His question again, "What's that in your hand?" I paused, my laces tangled around my fingers. A tiny seed of the smallest idea burrowed into my mind—an idea my dad and I later talked through.

Sitting around the table, we looked down at our feet and saw our worn, muddy running shoes. "What about a race?" we asked. And then we began to dream, realizing the Father had shown me the answer to His question, "What's that in your hand?"

"What about a race to raise money for kids in need in our hometown and the world?"

"What if we came alongside the vulnerable, the one with no advocate, the forgotten, the one crushed by oppression?"

"And what if we did more than raise money or create a fun event? What if we educated people on these kids' realities?"

It's incredible how our questions change when we realize what we have in our hands and throw it at Jesus' feet. What was once a cry of "What am I supposed to do," became "what if…" And these questions may not have put an end to the neglect in that overwhelmed Romanian orphanage, but in a small way, we helped build the Kingdom a little more.

Organizing a race like this felt completely ordinary. A team of students and adults came alongside my dad and me to lead registration and awards and the course. Our church provided the facility, tables, and a dozen other things for race day. And our community rallied around us, showing up in force on the chilly November morning of the race. All of that took extraordinary effort, of course. But this idea wasn't anything radical. The race didn't change the world. Yet it was a moment of dreaming bravely with the Father—well beyond my capabilities as a 15-year-old-girl. It was an answer to His question—what's that in your hand?

My answer was simple—my running shoes. Miles of running had worn them thin. Dirt caked the sides and bottom. The smell of sweat lingered inside. Some days, those shoes were the bane of my existence; other times they represented a sweet relief. But they were ordinary, smelly, worn, simple shoes—not totally unlike a staff.

Throw it at the Father's Feet

Can I be honest? I don't like depending on others. I'd rather figure out problems on my own and make things happen by myself. For most of my days, I have seen dependency as weakness—a sign that I couldn't handle whatever was being thrown my way. So I held others at arm's length as if to say, "I've got this. I don't need your help."

And I held God at arm's length too, relying on my own strength—as if the kinds of dreams I could accomplish on my own were the kinds of Kingdom-sized dreams He has. I believe He cares about our dreams and desires, whatever they are. But the kinds of dreams that move heaven and earth ask us to step a little deeper, trust a little more, and lean on Him completely.

This is why I love the staff. In Moses's hand, it was just a staff—unremarkable in every way. As hard as he might try, he could never make it turn into a snake on his own. He could hold it above his head as high as he could for as long as he wanted, and it wouldn't bring frogs or gnats or darkness. When Israel ached for water, Moses could have hit the rock with his staff until it broke, and no water would have gushed out. And when Israel fled Egypt, they wouldn't have crossed the Red Sea on dry ground if it were all up to Moses and his piece of wood.

The staff was only a staff until Moses threw it at the Father's feet. Then—and only then—did the Father transform it into a Kingdom-building tool. It wasn't all up to Moses.

Throughout Scripture, we see so many stories like his. Esther did the impossible to fight for God's people. The disciples travelled from town to town to share Jesus' message without taking money or supplies. Noah built an ark to save life on Earth. Each of these stories expected the supernatural. They depended on the Father. And if He didn't show up, they would experience betrayal, go hungry, look like fools, watch the mission fail, or even die.

And the same is true for us. Often the Father invites us to dream in that space where the creative and sacred collide—just beyond our capabilities. Created from His breath, He designed us to depend on Him. He sustains our very bodies. So is it any wonder that so often He leads us into Kingdom-building work that brings us to our knees at His feet—a place where we either have to cling to our lives or surrender to Him, rely on ourselves or depend on Him, worry about the results or worship the One who brings the victory.

It's in these moments—stuck in the tension of worry and worship—that I remember another moment in Israel's history. After wandering in the wilderness for forty years, the Lord allowed them to move into the promised land. First they had to make it past the fortress known as Jericho. Built with tall, thick walls, no one could conquer it.

Against all human wisdom, the Lord unveiled a plan that left everyone scratching their heads. Instead of charging into battle, catching the enemy by surprise, Joshua and his fighting men were to march around the city for seven days. Not only that, but they were to follow the most unlikely group—priests who would carry the Ark of the Covenant and blow ram's horns.

Do you see it? Swords and horses and muscles did not protect them as they charged into the unknown, pursuing an impossible dream. Worship was Israel's guard. The Lord's presence was their shield. Worry held no place in the army of God's people. Obedience and dependence marked their every move. Praise came before their victory. Worship was their very steps, and through it, the Father paved the way.

When we see what's in our hands, we can step into a dream bigger than we could accomplish on our own. When we choose worship over worry, dependence over self-reliance, He takes what's in our hand and leads us to a place we could never go on our own.

Moses's staff turns into a snake.

Israel's shout crumbles the walls of Jericho.

And in that place of surrender and total dependence, the Father uses those simple ordinary things we hold to do the miraculous. He doesn't just ask what's in our hand. He asks us to trust—to believe that He will do what seems impossible. He asks us to depend on Him even when our hearts beg to make things happen on our own, and He tells us to worship Him before victory comes.

He Wants our Yes

On a chilly November morning, I stood in front of a group of 200 runners, walkers, and their families. We huddled together outside of the church, just in front of the starting line. I stood in front of them—the leader of it all—and wondered if my nerves were as noticeable to them as they were to me. To be fair, most of them couldn't see me—the short, 15-year-old kid standing on my tiptoes. I gripped the bulky microphone with white knuckles and heard the crowd's chatter die down as I cleared my throat.

With all eyes on me, I thanked everyone for coming and explained what they would encounter on the course—stories and statistics, reminders of our immense responsibility to care for the vulnerable around us. I don't remember my entire speech. I just remember wishing I could pass the microphone to someone else and fade into the background.

But I couldn't. The Father had shown me what was in my hand, and He asked for something simple in return—my yes.

This yes didn't come easily. Fears, insecurities, questions, and doubts plagued my mind when the Father asked me to follow Him. And the same was true for Moses. Three different times he asked the Lord questions—thinly disguised ways of doubting the Father. It's not that we can't ask questions or have doubts, but when these stand in the way of our yes or make us believe a lie about who God is and who He created us to be, we doubt the very One who called us to come.

Moses tried everything to avoid saying yes. He pulled out every excuse he could think of, finally saying, "Lord, please! Send anyone else."[22]

The Lord, in His incredible goodness and love, didn't allow Moses to stay in this place of fear. He knew what Moses didn't. The Lord had created him for such a time as this. He only needed Moses to say "yes."

Friend, this is all He needs from you, too. He needs your yes, your willingness, your obedience. More times than not, the Father doesn't show us the entire plan. As we dream with Him—longing for more of the Kingdom of God on earth—He gives us glimpses. Like car headlights lighting the road at night, the Father shows us our very next step, and he asks us to say, "yes."

When I think of that 5K race, I see another step on my journey with the Father. This race wasn't a solution to the challenges vulnerable children face around the world.

Not by a long shot. But it was something. It was proof that I held something in my hand—something the Father wanted to use to build the Kingdom.

Friend, as we dream with the Father—bold, Kingdom-building dreams—He will ask us that question: "What's that in your hands?" Dreaming bravely means opening our clenched fists and seeing what the Father calls sacred. When He tells us, we summon our courage and throw these things at His feet, watching them turn into miracles. We depend on Him, choosing worship over worry, courage over fear.

And dreaming bravely begins and ends with that three letter word—the one that changes everything—yes. When we have the courage to say this simple word, we find the courage to dream bravely with the Father.

The Pause

The Father longs to dream with you. He longs to help you see the things He put in your hands in the beginning. In them, He longs to connect heaven and earth, and build His Kingdom. So before we dream with Him, I think we need to sit with the question He first asked from a burning bush.

What's that in your hand?

It's such an important question that determines how we dream. Will we let insecurities hold us back—believing we have little to offer? Or will we celebrate whatever we have in our hand, believing God can use it all?

Grab a pen and let's dive into this question together. At the top of the page, write the question, "What's that in my hand?" Think about your personality, gifts, talents, passions, hobbies. Think about the people the Father has put around you—your family, friends, neighbors. Write whatever comes to mind. Don't limit yourself or stop yourself from writing something that seems too ordinary. Write it all.

Now let's sit with another question—the one I asked after visiting the Romanian orphanage—"What am I supposed to do?" A close cousin to this question is the statement, "It's not supposed to be this way." Think about what makes your heart ache or fills you with sadness, holy anger, or a longing to make things right. Write whatever comes to mind. Remember, nothing is too big or too small.

Let's look over both lists. Let your eyes gaze over the words you wrote and ask the Father to unfold a Kingdom-building dream in your spirit. This may take a while. Sometimes dreaming with Him is a process. I had to begin in a place of believing that He wanted to dream with me, that He wanted to use me. Maybe this is where you need to begin. Then I needed to give myself permission to dream with Him, to take the time to be in His presence and hear from Him. For some of us, dreaming with the Father is new. So start where you are and allow the Holy Spirit to lead the process.

No matter where you find yourself as you dream with Him, remember that He wants your "yes." More times than not, this looks like saying "yes" to the very next thing

He's put in front of us rather than a giant, big-picture kind of dream. Whether or not you feel like He's given you a dream to step into, He has put something in your hand. Even now, He longs to use it. As you look at your list of things in your hand, ask the Holy Spirit to show you how He wants to use what's in your hand in this very moment.

And then, say "yes."

Say it to yourself and the Lord, and then share it with a close friend or family member.

All He needs are available and willing hearts that are ready to say "yes."

Your "yes" will look different from mine and mine different from yours, and that is beautiful. What matters is that we both say "yes" to whatever the Father asks us to step into.

So what is your "yes"?

Chapter 7

Your Story Matters

By Kristy Mikel

Making Shapes in the Sky

As a kid, I loved playing outdoors. We lived in the countryside on eighty acres of land with corn and soybean fields surrounding our small farm and a ditch with shallow water that ran along one side of the property. So as kids, my sisters and I had plenty of room for our imaginations to run wild. We were constantly outside, building a makeshift raft from scrap wood to sail across a shallow pond in the meadow, rigging a rope swing from a tree branch to jump across the bank of the ditch, or catching endless amounts of tadpoles swimming through the murky water.

One of my favorite memories as a kid was lying in the grass under the summer sun, staring up at the clouds in the sky and making shapes out of them as they passed by.

"That one looks like a lion," we squealed. "Oh, and there's a castle!"

Our imaginations ran wild—making shapes and telling stories. We felt inspired to dream, to create, to imagine without limitations. It was here so many of my dreams began—dreams to be a nurse, oceanographer, astronomer, author, mother, and the list goes on. I believed anything was possible. And like the clouds in the sky, my dreams shifted and changed through the years—each one based on new passions I discovered, unlimited in number.

If you had told a seven-year-old me making shapes out of clouds that one day I would live in Thailand and help run a ministry and business focused on empowering women, I would have thought it was a cool idea. But I never would have believed this is where I would be now.

Stepping into Someone Else's Dream

When I moved to Thailand, I knew I was coming alongside my teammate Kayla's dream. After all, it was with her that the dream of Braverly began—literally a dream the Lord gave her as she slept one night in January 2016. In it, she saw a giant mountain of corn seed stretching far above her head. As she stared at it, she heard the Lord ask her to open the floodgates of heaven and give resources to people to live out their divine purpose. This is a dream whose meaning the Lord has continued to uncover year after year.

When the Lord gave her the dream, she had been living in Thailand for over two years. She was partnering with a ministry focused on empowering locals on the Thailand and Myanmar border with education, humanitarian aid, vocational training, and more. This dream brought to mind several women and their families the Lord connected her to months before who were living in an abandoned mosque. Thinking of them, she wondered what it could look like to provide a space for their dreams to grow. And from this question came Braverly, a café and sewing center built to empower the dreams of these women— to be bakers, seamstresses, and businesswomen. Braverly would be a place for empowering their dreams to provide for their families and children.

It's an incredible dream, and I was excited to be a part of it. What an amazing opportunity to jump into something alongside my friend—empowering women, a passion we both shared. I had known the moment she asked me to join her, this was a step the Lord wanted me to take, but I had no idea how intimidating that step would be. Braverly was her story, her dream.

Looking back on it now, getting on the airplane and moving halfway across the world was the easy part. I was excited for a new adventure! The possibilities of Braverly seemed endless, and I wanted to be part of it! Yet as I moved forward, what surprised me most was the insecurity and fear that quickly rose to the surface.

"Kristy, you're not good enough, not godly enough to step into this dream," fear taunted.

"The Lord didn't give you the dream of Braverly," it continued. "So what do you have to offer?"

Kayla and I designed and created together, but in the back of my mind these comparisons grew. This dream didn't start with me. I knew very little about business. My mind struggled to keep up with our conversations about accounting and numbers. I barely liked coffee, yet here I was helping to build a coffee shop. Each day brought me face to face with more insecurities and fear. Stepping into this dream the Lord had given to Kayla, I didn't feel like I measured up. And as these comparisons took root in my heart, they invited shame into my story, dreams, and passions. I quickly fell into the trap of thinking that because my story was not like Kayla's, it was less significant and less worthy.

It was here—in this mindset—that shame was invited to make its home where it was never meant to be.

When Shame Takes a Seat at the Table

"You're not good enough," shame whispered from across the room sending ripples of fear and doubt down my spine.

It was becoming hard to focus as I sat at the table with Kayla in one of our regular business meetings. Troubleshooting problems was a normal part of our routine. Each day we asked questions about how we could grow the business. We had six employees—six women who looked to us for direction as we dove headfirst into seeing their dreams come to life. Our café doors opened to the community in November 2016, and we had a handful of customers each week. But we knew this wasn't going to be enough to sustain us. We had to find more ways to bring in business.

"Like you know what you're doing," came shame's mocking voice. I shifted uncomfortably in my seat.

"You don't know a thing about business," shame taunted. "You don't deserve to be here in this room. You're ill-equipped and in over your head. You're going to fail."

Kayla continued to share her thoughts—seemingly unaware of the third party sitting at the table with us. After all, it was me who'd invited him, and he existed in my mind.

Business seemed to come so naturally for her. I was amazed by how she knew what questions to ask and thankful for her understanding of business concepts. Without her we would drown! But I was completely lost as to how to help, feeling I had nothing of value to contribute. My mind didn't work like hers, and I was struggling to find my place.

Shame had been present for months, reminding me that what I was doing I'd never done before. I had no experience, and, because of that, my story did not belong.

This is what shame does.

When shame takes a seat at the table, it tells us our gifts and passions have no place. Shame tells us that what we are is not enough, that we should be something else. Shame takes the dreams of that seven-year-old girl under the summer sky and whisps away every cloud shouting, "That's not for you, maybe someone else! You could never do it!"

When shame takes a seat at the table, our comparisons are filled with lies, insecurities, and fears because shame never comes alone. When shame takes a seat at the table, fear receives an invitation to control our emotions, and doubt receives permission to infect our mind. Shame skews our vision as we look in the mirror, highlighting everything we are not. As we compare ourselves, our dreams, and our stories with others, we measure our worth by standards the Father never intended us to use. It's a rigged system in which we will always fall short because we will never live up to the image we have of the other person.

"Carry what I've given you," came the Lord's voice one night as I sat in tears in my home. "Let go of who you're not and serve this dream of empowering women with the gifts and passions I've given you!"

I am never going to be Kayla, and though the Lord gave her the dream of Braverly, He called me to be a part of it. But shame controlled my story, and unless I could learn to step out from under shame, I was never going to live as the unique creation the Lord designed me to be.

Saul Versus David: a Case Study in Shame

My story is not the first to encounter shame and certainly won't be the last. Shame has been whispering its lies from the beginning of time. From Adam and Eve hiding their nakedness from the Lord in the Garden of Eden to the woman we read about in Mark 5 who'd been bleeding for twelve years—shame has attempted to rewrite our stories for generations. One such story the Lord led me to in this season was the story of Saul and David.

Saul's story started off rocky. The people of Israel wanted a king—a real one they could see and follow, one who would unite their tribes and lead them forward. They wanted more than a God they couldn't see. Yet it was God's power that had split the sea and allowed the people to escape on dry ground from slavery in Egypt. It was the Lord who provided food from heaven and water from a rock as the people wandered in the desert for forty years. And it was the Lord who led them in victory over Jericho when the sound of their trumpets and shouts brought the walls crashing down, giving them possession of the promised land. The Lord had done it all! This would be a tough act to follow, but still the people insisted on a king. So God told the prophet Samuel to anoint Saul. But on the day of his anointing, Saul was nowhere to be found. Gripped by fear and wondering if he could be who the people desired, Saul hid among the luggage while they waited in anticipation for their new king!

What a place to start—hiding among luggage!

Saul had already invited shame and fear into his story—and his story had only begun. What began as a palace of possibility quickly turned into a place of contention. Placing his trust in other men rather than God, Saul made decisions based on those around him rather than remembering and honoring the unique calling the Lord gave him. And over time, Saul's disobedience caused the Lord to reject him as king. Saul grew weary and troubled. Fear had a hold of his mind and shame gripped his heart, so he commanded his servants to find him someone who could comfort him.

Enter David.

The youngest of eight brothers, David grew up as a shepherd boy who spent his days in the fields caring for his father's sheep. Each day he led them to newer, greener pastures to fill their hungry bellies. Watching over them with a careful eye, he kept them from wandering away. He warded off the attacks of lions and bears, determined to keep his father's flock safe. And with a harp in hand, he passed the time writing psalms and hymns to the God of Israel—remembering and celebrating the miraculous things He had done.

Hearing of David's musical talent, one of Saul's servants sent for him to play for the king. From a young age, David often visited Saul in the palace to soothe his soul with psalms and poems. David's gift made room for him in places few others would have the opportunity to enter. Praise of the Lord led David's life and with that came great courage rooted deeply within his soul. If the Lord was with him, who could be against him?

From the beginning of their stories, we can see a clear difference between where they placed their trust. One trusted that he would never be enough while the other knew that with God he had everything he needed. One trembled in fear when the Philistine army assembled for war near the Israelites' camp, distraught over who would face the giant Goliath. The other grabbed a sling and five small stones and marched out to meet him knowing the Lord would take down the giant through willing hands.

Shame altered Saul's story. And instead of reigning as the king he was anointed to be, Saul spent his days chasing after David, jealous of the ways the Lord used his gifts. Instead of building a kingdom of peace, Saul sowed a nation of discontentment—a people who were never satisfied and lost sight of the Lord. The ripples he sent out reconstructed the outlook of an entire nation. This is the power of shame's fierce tide.

The Ripples of Shame

When shame leads our story, the resulting ripples are destructive. Shame says "no" when the Father says "trust Me." Shame cries "I can't" when faced with the impossible. Shame believes "I'll fail" instead of taking a step toward courage. Shame leads us to care more about our safety and comfort than we do about our calling. Shame leads us to hide among the luggage instead of walking boldly toward the palace. Shame tells us to give up when things look impossible. Shame insists that someone else can do it better, so why even try?

Saul spread fear throughout the kingdom when their enemies came against them in war. Jealousy filled his palace as he watched David lead with courage and bring peace among the people. And insecurity led Saul's eyes to see only what he was not instead of standing on the truth of who God said he was. And it was shame that sent a man of promise to hide among the luggage.

And the result infected others.

Think of it this way. When you see someone who is afraid, it raises up in you a feeling of fear that wasn't there before. When you see someone respond in jealousy over how blessed another appears to be, it challenges your heart and mind to make similar comparisons. And when you see others give up in the challenges they face, it causes you to wonder if you should do the same.

Fear breeds fear. Jealousy breeds jealousy. Insecurity breeds insecurity. And shame breeds shame. Each one is destructive in its own right.

For Saul, allowing shame to direct his path caused him to miss the calling the Lord gave him. And when we miss the calling of the Lord in our lives, we miss the opportunity to give others courage, comfort, and hope as they live out their own brave stories. Instead, we live lives that ripple shame, defeat, and the deafening lies of "can't."

Your Courage Matters

As powerful as the ripples of shame, jealousy, insecurity, and fear are, greater still are the ripples of courage because they carry the power of Jesus Christ! Shame is not in His character, so it carries none of His power. But He is courageous, so our steps toward courage carry His great power.

When Saul's life came to a crashing halt, fear and shame were prominent among the rubble. Yet for David, the echoes of his courageous steps can still be heard throughout the world. Across every nation and in every language, David's willingness to step into God's call on his life led him to write many of the psalms, hymns, and songs we still sing in worship today!

Imagine for a moment if David had allowed shame to enter his story. Imagine if he had not understood the truth of his unique design. Imagine if he had bought into the lie that because he was merely a shepherd boy, he was incapable of leading people. This was a man who spent all day every day with a bunch of sheep. What did he know of battles against powerful armies? What did he know of protecting people who looked to him for an answer? Had shame entered his story, Goliath and the Philistine army might never have been defeated and the Lord's power might never have been displayed that day.

But David knew this truth. He gave it a seat at the table of his heart and wrote it down for us to know and one day believe. He was fearfully and wonderfully made, uniquely gifted and called by the Father, seen and known from the beginning of time. The Lord uniquely made him, unlike any of his brothers, and gifted him with exactly what he would need to lead people and bring them into a greater understanding of the Father's heart. This was to be a part of his story. And it was David's understanding of this truth that gave him the courage to bravely step into the places the Lord called him.

David may have never dreamed of being king of Israel while he watched his father's sheep in the field, but the Lord gifted him to step into that story. The Lord knew the gifts, the heart, the strength that David possessed. The Lord knew He needed a shepherd to lead Israel—someone who would care for them and defend them.

Friends, your courage matters!

Your courage carries the power of Christ into this world. Your courage shapes nations and generations. Your courage brings the kingdom to earth and sends light into darkness. We need your courage. We need your story.

Your Story Matters

Much like Saul, from the start of my story of living here in Thailand, shame dug its roots in, reminding me of everything I was not. Every moment I allowed fear and insecurity to speak, shame sprouted another root. The days when shame got a voice felt long and exhausting. Shame took my eyes and placed them firmly on myself—and because of shame, I missed out on the power of what Christ was doing and wanted to do all around me.

But thank God for grace.

Thank You, Father, that there is a grace over each and every one of our stories because You knew we'd need it as we learn to live as courageous sons and daughters who will stop at nothing to follow You.

Friends, just as David's story is uniquely his, your story is uniquely yours. Who God designed you to be is different than who He designed me to be. Your story is not my story, and my story is not yours.

Maybe it would benefit you to say that out loud. Wherever you find yourself, just speak it out—even if it's only a whisper. It's a truth we all need to hear, isn't it? A call to lay down our comparisons wrapped up in shame and embrace exactly who the Lord has designed us to be.

My story is not Kayla's story, just as her story is not mine. This dream may have begun with her and the Father, but He has led me here to it. He has uniquely gifted and designed me with something to add to Braverly's story— something that is uniquely part of my story. And if I can stop comparing myself to those around me, I can live brave, confident in who He says I am. I can dream bravely and step where the Lord leads. And the Lord can use my story to influence bravery in others—to challenge people to take their own brave steps with the Lord, confident in who they are, unafraid of where He will lead them.

While our stories may not be the same, we need each other's stories.

I need Kayla's story. It's through her story that I've come to know the Father in a new way—as a God who dreams with His children. And she needs my story to teach and challenge her in the way she knows the Lord. I need your story of courage to remind me, challenge me, and call me to continually walk boldly in mine. We need each other's stories: each one unique, each one important, each one a different reflection of the Father's heart.

The Pause

Your story matters! Often we settle for the lie that our story is not important, not enough, not...you fill in the blank, because our stories are messy, aren't they? They have high points and low points. Some days they're exciting, while others are miserably difficult and downright embarrassing. There are parts of our story we're proud of and others we wish we could forget. There are parts that inspire and parts we wish we could do differently. No story is perfect but each one is important. Hear that today, friend. Your story—all of it—is important.

I invite you to dive into your story.

Maybe shame is wrapped so tightly around your story that you're not sure where or how to begin. Yet our God is a redeeming God. He takes things the enemy means for evil and He turns them for good. Amen?

So let's start there, because we all have parts of our stories that could use some redeeming. I believe if we learn from our past mistakes, we can avoid future failures. So grab a pen and let's dive in below or in your journal.

As you consider where you are now—maybe thriving, maybe struggling—where does shame have a voice in your life? What has it been saying? Take time to journal your response.

Remember, shame thrives in secrecy, so today is about bringing shame into the light. As you look over what you've written, my next challenge to you is an uncomfortable one, but it's a step I believe in your ability to take.

Who is a trusted voice in your life—a friend, a family member, a co-worker, a pastor, a mentor? Who is someone you feel you're able to share with honestly? My challenge to you is to embrace vulnerability—bring shame into the light and share with someone you trust about what it has spoken over you. There is freedom to be found unlike we have ever experienced before. Shame, lies, and fear cannot survive the light. In the light, we can finally see the way forward. So be brave and share your story with someone else you trust. Let it be a holy moment that the Lord can use to speak His truth.

Secondly, I want to invite you on a journey into the Psalms. David penned over one hundred of them to remind us of the Father's heart and His call and invitation to us, His children. The Psalms are filled with battle cries against shame, fear, insecurity, and doubt. They are filled with praises and reminders of how the Lord has been so faithful. They are pictures of hope and life redeemed and restored. And they are filled with declarations of embracing the Father's love for us and carrying it out into the world!

Here's my challenge: dive in.

Maybe you want to commit to reading a Psalm each morning and each night. Or maybe pick some specific Psalms to dive deeper into their meaning. Consider learning about some of the more popular Psalms—Psalm 1, 23, 46, 100, or 139. Or maybe, like David, you want to pen a psalm of your own—a prayer to the Lord, a declaration of His work in your life, a battle cry to carry forward as you continue to live out your own brave story! Take the journey, friend. Allow God's Word to speak and move in your life—to lead you to take another courageous step forward.

Your story matters. The ripples you send into the world have the ability to shape and transform hearts and nations. So take your next brave step. See what's in your hand and how the Lord has uniquely gifted you with it and boldly live out your story for the world around you to see!

I will worship you, Yahweh, with extended hands as my whole heart erupts with praise! I will tell everyone everywhere about your wonderful works! I will be glad and shout in triumph. I will sing praise to your exalted name, O Most High. Psalm 9:1-2, TPT

Chapter 8

Courageous Communion

By Kate Berkey

Fighting for Courageous Communion

A chapter about connection feels sort of out of place in the most connected time in history. We hold the world at our fingertips, but somehow, we pull farther apart. We send texts and tweets in our rush from here to there, trapped in life's frantic pace. Our posts on social media tell curated stories with filters and good lighting. We say we're connected but could it be that all of this is an attempt to fill the void of that which we most long for: personal connection?

I wrote an entire chapter about this and scrapped it all. Each paragraph made me gag. They were shallow responses—like putting a band aid on a bullet wound. As true as it was, the chapter offered nothing of substance, especially to a world crying out for our hearts' longing—communion.

But none of this is new. So often, we wake up lonelier and more afraid than yesterday. Anxiety plants seeds in our minds and traps us in an endless cycle. Panic and fear hold us behind iron bars, and we feel so alone. If only we looked to our left and right, we would notice the men and women standing beside us bearing their own burden called fear.

If we're honest, we've all experienced a bit of this loneliness and isolation—aching for belonging and a group we can call "our people." The Father wired us for connection and created us for community which is the tangible expression of communion.

As followers of Jesus, we think of communion as the sacred act of breaking bread and drinking wine, but communion is much more. Communion is a complicated mixture of what we long for and what fills us with fear. It comes from the Greek word *koinōnia*.[23] At its core is fellowship, community, and sharing. It is intimate and vulnerable, selfless and sacrificial.

Think of the Garden of Eden. In the beginning, God and Adam walked together, named animals, and enjoyed creation. Life was communion with God. After a while, He said, "It's not good for Adam to be alone," so the Father created Eve. Human beings doing life together became the second form of communion.

After sin entered the world, a chasm separated us from God and each other. Throughout history, humans have attempted to fill this void with the fix of the day. Today, our cure is distractions and idols and poor replacements for connection. All of it becomes an attempt to pad our comfort zone. As we lean into these artificial substitutes, we grow more and more lonely and afraid. We forget that we share courage in koinōnia.

The night Jesus walked to His death, He gathered His disciples for communion. At the table, they broke bread and loved one another. In the garden Jesus cried out to the Father, spilling drops of blood on the very ground He created. Greatly troubled and distressed, Jesus said, "Take this cup from me!" God incarnate felt terrified. He was alone, and He wanted out. Jesus needed His people that night, but in their humanity, they let Him down. He needed their courage, but His friends slept through His pain.

In communion, we share courage. It starts with the Father and spreads to each other. We share it in intimate, vulnerable, messy life connected to life. Here, we remember that we're not alone. We never were and never will be.

I'm not here to convince you that community is important. Deep down, I think we all know our incredible need for it. This chapter isn't a step-by-step guide on how to build relationships and experience koinōnia with others. I don't think it's a one-size-fits-all thing. Rather, the pages that follow are a call to communion—intimate, vulnerable, messy, persistent connection.

Fighting for authentic, courageous communion with the Father and others could be one of the most important battles of our lives because when we find ourselves in our own Garden of Gethsemane moments, we will need the courage of both to whisper those brave words, "Your will be done, not mine."

His Last Moments of Communion

Jesus knew His life would come to this—the Passover table with His twelve disciples. Passover marks a moment in Israel's history. Far from home and enslaved by the Egyptians, the Israelites cried out to the Father for rescue, and in a final plague, He brought death to the first-born sons in the homes without the blood of the lamb on their door. Year after year, Israel marked this moment of sacrifice—the one that spared them from death and delivered them into freedom.

On this Passover, Jesus walked toward a similar sacrifice. This time, though, He was the lamb. His blood stained the doorframe, marking the lives of God's people. It's the reason He became a man—God incarnate.

That night, Jesus seemed different. The disciples noticed a heaviness in His voice, actions, and demeanor. Maybe it was the pressure of life in the spotlight or the constant death threats that weighed Him down. Maybe He needed to pause or pray. He'd been talking about death nearly every day for the last few weeks, but His disciples didn't understand. No one could stop Jesus on His quest to Jerusalem, and His disciples struggled to comprehend His words and actions.

He'd loved His disciples every day He was with them, and now He loved them to the very end. So He wrapped a towel around His waist and washed their feet, proving the Kingdom was more backward than they knew. He broke bread and served them wine—pouring out the new covenant before them. With every breath, He taught, encouraged, and gave them glimpses of the Kingdom.

Before His death scattered them, they gathered around a space that nourished them. Each had a seat at the table—despite their shortcomings and mishaps. Each had a place to belong. And Jesus delighted in this moment of communion with them, because even though they would let Him down, they were His friends, His family, His people—the ones with whom He experienced koinōnia.

After dinner, the group walked to the Garden of Gethsemane. The end was coming closer and closer, and Jesus felt it. Dread overwhelmed Him and brought Him to His knees in prayer. With three of His disciples only a stone's throw away, He bared his soul to the Father. Sweat and drops of blood spilled on the ground.

"'Abba, Father,' He cried out, 'everything is possible for you. Please take this cup of suffering away from me.'"[24]

His breath came sharper now. Heart pounding in His chest, He swallowed hard. Jesus knew this was the road He needed to walk, and He delighted in knowing what the new covenant would bring to all of humanity. But none of this took away the fear, dread, or terror from bearing the weight of sin.

He was alone—the disciples asleep behind Him. But communion didn't depend on these men. Taking a deep breath, leaning hard into the Holy Spirit, Jesus dug into the courage found in communion with the Father and said those ten brave words, "Yet I want your will to be done, not mine."[25]

If ever He needed to borrow courage from others, it was on the walk to the cross. But that night, all of Jesus' disciples abandoned Him. One condemned Him to death. Another denied knowing Him three times. Fear scattered the rest. Still, He said, "Yes."

For Jesus, communion was much more than what He shared among His disciples. Its roots buried deep into the Father and became tangible in His relationships with others. So while Jesus prayed alone that night, He was never alone, and the communion He shared with the Father didn't begin in that moment. It started thirty-three years earlier—a baby in a manger, a child teaching in His Father's house, a man withdrawing to fast and pray, a Savior who loved until the very end with the Father's love.

On the night Jesus died, He shared communion with both His disciples and the Father. Jesus served His friends. They ate together and talked about the Kingdom, betrayal, and events to come. He shared the table with all of them, even the ones who would abandon Him. And that night, Jesus spent His last moments as a free man communing with Abba, Father—the One who had given Him a task that seemed impossible. With courage He found in communion with both, He walked toward the cross, and our world was changed forever.

Trading Scraps for the Feast

Sometimes I think we embrace a shallow idea of community. So often, our picture of community isn't bad; it's just incomplete—like settling for scraps in the kitchen when a feast sits on the table.

I've walked through seasons of fighting against community and choosing self-protection. Those days, I rooted myself in isolation and built a brick wall around my heart. Other seasons, I embraced community with my whole heart. I walked into vulnerability and invited others to do the same. We did life together, until things got too messy or we moved away or drifted apart.

We've all faced the temptation to walk away. Sometimes that feels easier or more comfortable. The reality is seasons and relationships change. Things happen beyond our control and our community changes, but the temptation to choose comfort over persistence is different.

Communion is messy. The more I look at the communion table and the communion garden, the more I recognize this. They're marked by friendship and courage, but we can't miss the more challenging side of communion because we will face both sides. We'll gather our friends around the table, but sitting with us could be someone who will hurt us. We'll serve our community and also fight the temptation to one-up one another. We'll rally the courage to invite others into our deepest pain and vulnerability, only to experience their complete indifference or inability to hold our story.

But that doesn't mean we avoid it. The challenging parts aren't a case for isolation and self-protection. They are an acknowledgement of reality. We have to lean into the uncertainty of communion to experience the richness and courage that comes when we do it right.

Communion happens around the table. It happens over bread and wine. And it happens in the Garden of Gethsemane when we face fears and let out our tears. Despite all of the challenges and obstacles, we fight for it. We fight for what Jesus experienced with the Father and Holy Spirit. It's here we find the deepest, most fulfilling courage. And we fight for what Jesus cultivated with those twelve imperfect, messy, broken disciples. It's here that we borrow and share courage among each other.

So we need to set aside our ideas about communion or at least be willing to exchange or expand them. The scraps in the kitchen aren't bad, but a feast awaits us on the table. It is messy and complicated—a mixture of incredible and uncomfortable, beautiful and painful. So come to the table, and walk to the garden, because in these places we will find true koinōnia and rich courage.

Communion Love

Each of the Gospel writers carries a unique perspective, and I especially love John's. So often he sees things differently, and I think this is beautiful. When he recounts

Passover, he doesn't talk about the bread or the wine—the body broken, the blood spilled. Instead, He remembered a towel and dirty feet and an act of service—the full expression of Jesus' love.

John 13:1 (NLT) says, "Before the Passover celebration, Jesus knew that His hour had come to leave this world and return to His Father. He had loved His disciples during His ministry on earth, and now He loved them to the very end."

Isn't that beautiful? He loved them the entire time they were together—even to the very end. In an act that felt so backward, Jesus took off His robe and wrapped a towel around His waist. Kneeling on the floor, He went to one disciple and then the next, washing the dirt and grit from their feet.

Other translations of this verse write that Jesus showed them the "full extent of His love." The full extent of His love was messy and vulnerable. It meant stripping down to a towel and scrubbing dirty feet. It brought Him to His knees—taking a position of humility rather than power. Later, the full extent of His love led Jesus to the cross—the ultimate sacrifice for those He loved.

In this story, there's a detail we can't miss.

Jesus excluded no one.

He knew Judas would condemn Him to death, Peter would deny Him three times, and the rest of the disciples would flee in fear. And He knew His enemies would torture and kill Him for crimes He never committed.

Despite this, He slipped off His robe and tied a towel around His waist. Peter's denial didn't change Jesus' love, so He knelt in front of Peter and took off his sandal. He washed one foot and then the other. And then He moved to Judas—the one who traded Jesus' life for thirty pieces of silver. His was the ultimate betrayal. Was Jesus' throat tight with grief as He scrubbed the dirt from Judas's feet? Did fear and anger fill His heart? Did tears threaten to slip down His cheeks?

I believe Jesus' love for Judas was also constant until the very end because Judas was an image bearer. I might be wrong about His love, but I know that on the night He died, Jesus still included Judas in everything—the communion supper, the communion foot washing, the communion table.

This is where koinōnia starts and ends—love.

It's extravagant and gracious. When Jesus broke the bread and served the wine, He served it to everyone. Jesus' love didn't exclude or restrict. His disciples didn't have to be a certain person or believe a certain theology. They were fishermen and tax collectors. They were ordinary, unschooled men, but because of Jesus's love, they experienced communion with Him.

Too often we limit our community. I'm not saying you should allow everyone in your inner circle. Nor am I saying that we should stay in abusive, damaging relationships. Not even Jesus did these things.

But His community included those outside of His political or theological alignment. He—a rabbi—sat with tax collectors and prostitutes and those He delivered from demons. Day after day, He showered grace on His disciples. And even though He knew they would end up betraying Him, He fought for them; He never gave up on them.

Luke captures this beautiful moment between Peter and Jesus in Luke 22:31-32 (NLT). He says, "Simon, Simon, Satan has asked to sift each of you like wheat. But I have pleaded in prayer for you, Simon, that your faith should not fail. So when you have repented and turned to me again, strengthen your brothers."

Communion lives and breathes in love—extravagant, moving love. This love doesn't just create space for everyone at the table. It continually sets a place for others even when they disappoint us. Even when we fall short, koinōnia fights for the other. It believes the best about the other. It never gives up. It endures through every circumstance.

And this love serves one another—even those who have hurt us or may hurt us. When John writes about the full extent of Jesus' love, he tells a story of God incarnate kneeling on the ground, washing the dirt from the disciples' feet. This love isn't self seeking. It serves the other, even when it feels uncomfortable or messy or backward. And now, He leans in close and asks us to do the same with those around us.

It's the kind of love we see in 1 Corinthians 13. This love is patient and kind. It's not jealous or boastful or proud or rude. It doesn't exclude or keep any record of being wronged. Love doesn't get caught up in petty things—

disagreements or arguments or differences. It doesn't rejoice in injustice or retribution or join in gossip. Love rejoices when truth wins out, when the other succeeds, when joy touches the lives of those around us. It never gives up or loses faith in others. It's always hopeful and endures through every circumstance. Love wraps a towel around its waist and serves.

Loving others like this is daunting. We'll mess up. We'll fall short, and others will disappoint us too. But love within koinōnia means continuing to set the table for and serve those around us, because Jesus first did this for us when we least deserved it.

Communion Vulnerability

C. S. Lewis has this profound quote in his book *The Four Loves*. He writes, "To love at all is to be vulnerable. Love anything and your heart will be wrung and possibly broken. If you want to make sure of keeping it intact you must give it to no one, not even an animal."[26]

Vulnerability is hard, isn't it? You know it when you feel it—that uneasy pit in your stomach, your quickened heartbeat, sweaty palms, a mouth that's as dry as a desert. For a lot of us, vulnerability feels like weakness. It's something we'd rather run from than toward. But it exists all around us—when we share our story or invite friends over for dinner or allow others to see the real us. It's in love and grace, and whether we realize it or not, vulnerability is the lifeblood of every relationship we value and treasure.

Even Jesus embraced vulnerability. This truth is so easy for us to forget. Sometimes, I imagine Jesus as a stoic man casually walking through life, healing the sick and wounded, teaching the crowd in a monotone voice. In reality, Jesus lived in the emotional exposure of vulnerability day after day. When His friend died, Jesus wept. In anger, He overturned tables in the temple. On the night He met death, He felt terrified. And He never hid any of this from His friends.

Jesus welcomed vulnerability rather than feared it. Day after day, He risked what others might think of Him and cultivated a beautiful communion with the Father and His disciples. He invited the disciples into His pain and joy. He shared with them, inviting them into intimate koinōnia like they had never before experienced. Vulnerability was and still is a risk worth taking.

Vulnerability in communion with others means we don't have to hide or avoid hard things. Like Jesus with the disciples, we share it all in trusting relationships and invite others to do the same. We're not meant to share this kind of vulnerability with everyone, but too often we share it with no one. We're too afraid. We hold vulnerability at arm's length, calling it weakness. It fills us with fear, uncertainty, and uneasiness, and so we run from it. Your story and struggles and joys deserve to fall on the people you trust—those who fight for you.

Friends, I would venture to say that we struggle to practice vulnerability with one another because we can't bring ourselves to be vulnerable with the Father first.

I struggle in this fight to be vulnerable with the Father, and I feel silly for saying that. He's God. He knows me more deeply and fully than I could ever know myself. He knows my thoughts and motives and the deepest and darkest corners of my life. Why can't I be honest with Him? Why can't I tell Him my needs, my emotions, my questions, my doubts? He already knows them, but there's something profoundly sacred about acknowledging them in His presence.

Vulnerability in communion with the Father means that we don't have to pretend. We can embrace our weaknesses because they are what make us human. His grace covers them; His power is made perfect in our weakness. We find our courage and strength in the Father. We don't have to hide. The Father cares about our needs and the desires of our hearts—no matter how big or small. And when we can sit with these truths, with the unending, extravagant love of the Father, we can sit with ourselves—our deeply broken, imperfect, vulnerable selves. When we embrace vulnerability with the Father, we can find the courage to do the same with others.

Vulnerability is always a risk. But to avoid it is to avoid love. To avoid it is to eat scraps in the kitchen when a feast sits at the table.

"Come," Jesus says, "join me in vulnerability. It is your strength, not your weakness."

Communion Pain and Persistence

Deep, thriving, long-lasting relationships are rare. They are something to treasure and hold with gratitude. In my life, I've experienced very few of these relationships—ones that have thrived for five or ten or fifteen years. These relationships are sacred.

As a kid, I met one of these friends, and for twenty years, we have experienced beautiful, messy communion. She's my middle-of-the-night person, the one I call when everything feels like it's falling apart or when I get the very best news. She's my laugh-until-you-cry friend and also one of the few people with whom I never apologize when the tears of pain and sadness slip. Over the years, my mind and heart have treasured the most vivid memories of conversations about life and relationships and Jesus and where we thought we would be in five years—communion at its best.

Until life got messy. Differences cracked our once common ground. Disagreements and hurts and messy struggles felt more common than the moments of carefree laughter. The friendship that sustained me stood on shaky ground, and this reality felt like a punch to the gut. Honestly, some days it felt easier to walk away, to blame our changing communion on changing seasons and personalities. Sometimes this happens. Life and relationships have seasons, but there was something deeper the Father longed for us to lean into—persistence.

And so we do. We persist with a whole lot of love and grace, and we experience a different depth of communion.

Within communion, vulnerability and love have an incredible power to develop intimacy with one another. Relationships grow deeper and deeper roots when we love without condition and exception, but I think there's another side to communion that we can't miss. It holds beauty and challenge in tension. It is pain and persistence.

Throughout Jesus' entire life, He confronted the effect of people's mistakes and mishaps. He constantly challenged the disciples' faith. He rebuked the religious leaders. He called people to a higher calling—to Kingdom living.

On the night He died, He knew the disciples would betray and deny Him. Those He'd loved so fiercely would flee from Him. Communion is sometimes so painful, and yet, Jesus persisted. His merciful kindness and grace for others are the foundation for His communion. Without it, I think He would have given up.

Friends, we are messy, aren't we? We're broken, imperfect people who fall short time and time again. In communion with one another, we walk a fine line. How far is too far; when is it okay—healthy even—to walk away? Jesus once told one of His followers to forgive others seven times seventy times—that is, over and over and over again, more times than we can remember and keep track of. Other times, He warned the crowds of the hypocrisy of the religious; it was a warning against communion with them. As followers of Jesus, we hold this idea of grace and persistence in tension with the genuine reasons we should walk away from communion with others.

And yet on the night Jesus died, He'd already forgiven Peter for the three times he would deny knowing Jesus. As He hung on the cross—put to death by those He came to love and save—Jesus cried out to the Father, "Father, forgive them, for they don't know what they are doing."[27]

Communion persists even in pain, and pain always comes. To ignore it is to ignore reality. Those we cultivate communion with will disappoint us. They will let us down. We will step into love and vulnerability—giving so much of ourselves to others—and sometimes, they will fall short. Sometimes we will too.

Courageous communion extends grace and forgiveness. It persists and fights for the other with truth, trust, and love because we follow Jesus' example. Despite the pain that communion caused Him, it was worth it. So He offered endless amounts of grace. He persisted without exception. So should we.

My Courageous Communion

Tears spilled from my eyes—the kind that come from big, uncontrollable sobs—and I had long since given up trying to stop them. Surrounded by people who had transformed my life, I let the tears fall, overflowing from a cup that once felt empty.

Breathing deeply, I remembered the words the Father had spoken to me when I first arrived in Thailand and met these people. He'd said, "It's time to tear down the walls around your heart brick by brick." The memory of that moment still brings tears to my eyes because I remember the journey. I remember the refining and chipping away. And I remember who I was inside those brick walls.

When I stepped off that rickety propellor plane in Mae Sot, I came raw and insecure and isolated from others—ready to prove myself to my team. Isn't that how the unhealthiest stories start—eager to prove ourselves? Over time, I would learn that in authentic, courageous communion we have nothing to prove. We live and rest in love.

In just nine months, my team helped me relearn the beauty of vulnerability. They'd offered me a safe place to land and invited me to share my story and struggles with honesty and courage. This group became the family I didn't know I needed. And as my communion with the Father grew deeper and stronger, so did my communion with them.

On the day with all the tears, I was saying goodbye, and it was breaking my heart. The Lord had made it clear—I needed to go back to the US, and the anxiety of this move kept me awake at night. This season was ending, but I didn't really understand why. I didn't know what I was stepping into. I didn't know when I would see my Thailand family again. I didn't know when I would once again experience the beautiful communion we had shared.

Day after day, I wrestled with the Lord. I had given up trying to hide my tears from my team, so they saw the struggle, and they held my hand in it. As we gathered around the table that night, we experienced communion—honesty and vulnerability, grace and love. They persisted with me, held me up when I felt exhausted, and gave me the courage to get back on that rickety propellor plane bound for the US.

In true communion, this community walked with me hand in hand.

A few years earlier, I had run the roads of Chicago with my dad in the Chicago Marathon. We'd trained for months—enduring heat and storms and blistered feet. Months of training culminated in this one race, but that day everything went wrong. My body turned on me, and my dad and I walked for ten miles. The physical pain, mental struggle, and emotional disappointment of the race crushed me. Every aid station was a temptation to quit, to drop out, to catch a ride in a warm, dry SUV. I was ready to give up, and I would have quit. I didn't have the courage to continue.

But my dad did.

So we kept going. We walked mile after mile, the wind from Lake Michigan freezing our sweat. As we turned the last corner and saw the finish line, my dad took my hand, and we ran the last hundred feet hand-in-hand.

That day I wasn't very strong. I wasn't very brave or courageous. My heart and mind and body begged for relief. "Give up!" They said. But my dad told me to be courageous. He told me that courage is persisting when everything falls apart. Friends, I had no bravery of my own that day. I clung to my dad's courage, and it was enough to propel me across the finish line.

This is communion.

It's walking hand in hand through life—the triumphs and hardships. It's anchoring ourselves to the Father and the people He's put around us. It's taking each other's hand with love and vulnerability and persistence and helping each other courageously walk a little further.

Communion Courage

There's this incredible moment in Acts 4. It's after Jesus went back to the Father, and the Holy Spirit filled the Upper Room. Peter boldly preached to the crowd, and the early church found its beginnings. So many good and beautiful things were happening among the believers, but they also met resistance. In chapter four, we see Peter and John on trial before the same council who had sentenced Jesus to death just a few weeks earlier.

Peter, the one who had denied knowing Jesus, stood in front of the religious leaders and, filled with the Holy Spirit, proclaimed the truth about Jesus. This was the man who sunk beneath the waves and hid after the crowd crucified Jesus. But he was different now, and the council noticed the change.

Verse 13 says, "The members of the council were amazed when they saw the boldness of Peter and John, for they could see that they were ordinary men with no special training in the Scriptures. They also recognized them as men who had been with Jesus" (NLT).

Again and again, Jesus' refrain to the disciples was courage. He called Peter to walk on the waves because He believed in His ability to come and called him courageous.

He sent the disciples out in Luke 10 and empowered them to do what they'd seen Him do. On the night He predicted Peter's denial, Jesus called him back before Peter had even walked away. He did all of this because He truly believed in His disciples. This belief, this empowerment, this relationship within communion sparked courage in His disciples well after Jesus returned to the Father.

This happens in communion. We share courage. We borrow courage. We find courage. Remember the moment between Jesus and the Father in the garden? Jesus was deeply distressed; the weight of the night ahead terrified Him. And yet He said those beautiful words, "Your will be done not mine." This courage came in koinōnia.

I'm not always great at koinōnia. I desire intimacy and also fear the vulnerability it takes to get there. I've experienced seasons of beautiful communion with the Father and with others. I've stepped into true vulnerability with them and invited them to do the same with me. Other times, I've built tall, brick walls around my heart—sort of like the walls around Jericho. I've traded communion for isolation, believing I was protecting my heart from the hurt that can come when we love others deeply. In these seasons, I've found myself lonelier and more afraid than ever before. I'm still learning. I'm still growing. Some days I get it right, and other days I fall short. And I'm sure the same is true for you.

Communion is a practice, but it's something we need to fight for. Someday we will face our own garden moment, and in communion we'll find the courage to take another step on our journey.

The Pause

What a gift it is to practice communion. Let's not miss that. This is a practice—a daily decision to step deeper into our relationship with the Father and with each other. As we make the bold decision to enter communion, we will share courage. We'll find courage in the Father and borrow the courage of other believers.

Communion begins with the Father. It seems so fitting that we began this journey talking about the extravagant love of the Father. Here, in His love and communion, we find the rest and courage our soul needs.

The Father is not far away. He is so very near, and He longs to share communion with you. As we step into our final Pause, grab a pen. It's a gift to experience communion with the Holy Spirit. Take a moment to ask Him to speak as you dive into the next few pages.

Think about your communion with the Father. What does it look like now? Have you allowed Him to show you the full extent of His love—to wash your feet, to serve you? Have you embraced vulnerability in relationship with Him? Allow the Holy Spirit to speak to you. In the space below or in your journal, write your thoughts and reflections on your communion with the Father. As you pray, lean into vulnerability with Him, telling Him what is on your heart.

Think about your communion with others. Who is your tribe? Do you have people you love and serve and allow them to do the same for you? Do you avoid vulnerability in relationships with others? Is the Father asking you to persist more in a relationship with a specific friend? Write your thoughts and reflections on your communion with others.

What does it look like to take steps deeper into communion with the Father and with others? Write out specific next steps, dreams you have for communion, and prayers for your tribe.

Now let's take another step. Who is one person or maybe even a few people in your tribe who need to hear about these dreams and prayers? I want to encourage and challenge you to step deeper into communion with them by sharing what the Father has stirred in your heart.

All our brave living and dreaming will mean nothing if we cannot live and dream with others and encourage bravery in others. So let's step into courage and step into communion. Let's live brave, dream bravely, and influence bravery together.

Conclusion

Friend, we've made it to the end, but this isn't the end of the journey. In so many ways, this is just the start. From here, we will have days full of stops and starts, steps forward and backward. We'll mess up and miss the mark and ask for forgiveness more times than we can count. You and I will learn humility as we dare to live brave, dream bravely, and influence bravery. More than that, we will learn more about the God who calls us daughters.

That's what this has all been about. Our world is full of books and Ted Talks and videos and motivational speeches about courage. We just don't need more of those things. We need more of the Father, Son, and Holy Spirit. More than anything else, our prayer is that you would encounter our wild and wonderful God a little more every day. And as you encounter Him more, our prayer is that you would embrace the name He gives you as His daughter.

Friend, there's a reason we ended with a chapter on communion and community. As we travel through life, we desperately need each other. We need to lean on the Father, and we need to lean on the people He has put in our life. So as you walk with courage, walk with others. Welcome vulnerability as a friend rather than a foe.

And here's the last thing we will leave you with.

Your story matters. Your courage matters. The decisions you make about your life today have the power to shape the generations that follow you. They have the ability to shape the nations. Your brave steps today will leave a lasting imprint for others to follow.

May you live brave—choosing courage in the everyday ordinary and extraordinary moments.

May you dream bravely—dreaming beyond your limits and capabilities knowing that the Father is more than capable.

May you influence bravery—sparking courage in others who never dreamed it was possible.

May you be a woman marked by the Father, Son, and Holy Spirit, a woman who dares to live with courage.

The Braverly Charge

Today, I will live brave.

Fear has no foothold to control my decisions.

And shame has no authority to plague my mind.

I live from a place of rest in the Father's love.

He calls me daughter, and I have access to everything He has because I am in His family.

I live from a place of courage because He calls me courageous.

So I will come, because He says I can!

Today, I will dream bravely.

Fear does not limit what I can accomplish with the Father.

And shame won't hold me back from dreaming bold, daring dreams.

I am a woman who knows my place, and it is found in the Kingdom alongside Jesus.

The Father calls me to dream with hands wide open, surrendered to Him.

He sees what my hands hold and asks me for my yes.

And I will say this yes with courage!

Today, I will influence bravery.
Fear will not hold me back in insecurity.
And shame will not keep me hidden in the shadows of comparison and lies.
My story is unique—unlike any other the Father is writing—and He says it is good.
So I will declare the goodness of the Lord through my brave story.
My community has the power to infuse me with courage and I the same for them.
So I will treasure my community.

Today, I will be Braverly.
Part of a community of women around the world, we journey together.
Each day we have a decision to make.
Today, tomorrow, and the next day, we choose to
Live brave
Dream bravely
And influence bravery

We are Braverly.

Acknowledgments

I f it takes a village to raise a child, it took an entire city to turn this small idea of a dream into a reality. And without this tribe, we would still be talking about this idea of a book.

To our Outpour Family Foundation team, we owe you Thursdays from now until eternity. Thank you for letting us sneak away from Mae Sot for writing retreats and writing days. Thank you for carving out space within already crowded schedules, for praying with us and for us, for believing so deeply in the dream the Father gave us. Without you all, the busyness of life would have crowded out the time it takes to create something like this.

To Kayla—our fearless leader—thank you for creating space for Kristy to step away from Braverly to write. Thank you for believing in this dream so fiercely that you convinced Kate to quit her full-time job and follow Jesus to Thailand. You are the picture of Braverly, and we love you so much.

To Miriam Surin, you are the woman we thought of time and again as we wrote the pages of this book. Your love for the Father, for your Karen people, and for the oppressed and marginalized inspires us daily. Because of your tireless work, we continue to have the proper paperwork to live and work in the beautiful country of Thailand in the first place. Thank you for the ways you help a group of farangs follow Jesus in Thailand.

To Boss—our fearless Thai teacher, translator, and book critic—thank you for your patience no matter how many times we mispronounce Thai words. Thank you for helping a group of Americans navigate the cultural and language nuances in Mae Sot. Your unrelenting honesty, kindness, and friendship mean the world to us.

To our incredible supporters. Without you, we would not be able to hold this book in our hands. From your prayers to your words of encouragement to your dollars, we are so grateful for all the ways you've invested in this project. We were faithful to write words on these pages, but you were faithful to help it become a physical, tangible object. The Kingdom of God is being built because of you!

To our entire team of editors and publishing masters at Morgan James Publishing, thank you! Thank you for taking a chance on a few unknown authors. Thank you, Terry Whalin, for believing in our book more than we did some days! We absolutely could not have done this without you.

To the Berkey crew, leaving you all for nearly a year to live in a country 9,000 miles away was one of the most challenging things the Lord has asked me to do. Yet you all made it strangely easy because of your unending love and support. Thank you for your constant encouragement. To Mom and Dad, thank you for never letting me quit—for being my cheerleaders every day. To Finley and Maeve, you two are Braverly; this book is for you, loves.

To the Mikel clan, I feel like you've sacrificed so much, and I can never say thank you enough! Thank you for standing by me and supporting me, for encouraging me to go wherever the Lord leads, even if that means living 9,000 miles away. To Mom and Dad, thank you for raising me with hands and arms wide open—for cheering me on and challenging me toward obedience to the Father every day. To the Prenkert tribe, thank you for pouring more into my life than you could ever know. Katylynn, Moses, Kiki, & Mali, I thank God every day for the brave lives He's leading you to live. And to Amy and Joy, you're two blessings I never saw coming. I see in you a mom and daughter who are nothing short of the heartbeat of what it means to be Braverly—deep, deep love to you both as you continue to embrace your own brave journeys.

To the women of Braverly sewing center and café, you are Braverly. This book is for you. We love you!

About the Authors

Kate Berkey is a writer and missionary in Chicago, Illinois, where she serves refugee and immigrant families on the north side of the city. She has worked in ministry and discipled other believers for nearly ten years and has served in six countries in short and long-term missions. As a writer, she has published numerous devotionals and articles for publications around the United States. Kate is all about family and deeply desires to help others find belonging in the family of the Kingdom of God. More than anything else, she longs to walk women home to the heart of the Father—their creator and sustainer. Kate is a lover of being on the water, running on Lakefront Trail, and gathering dear friends around the table.

Kristy Mikel is the co-director of Braverly, a ministry in Mae Sot, Thailand, where she has lived and served since 2016. Prior to moving to Thailand, Kristy spent over sixteen years in ministry and has served in seventeen different nations through short-term and long-term missions. As she partnered with the discipleship efforts of the local church, discipled women in a red-light district in Kenya, and became a learner of new cultures, Kristy cultivated a heart for the nations and a passion for seeing that same heart cultivated in others. Her experiences, both in the US and abroad, have given her unique perspectives, insights, and stories as she walks alongside women of all ages in their journey to the Father. Kristy is a daughter, sister, missionary, and carries a deep passion for empowering women worldwide. She's a fierce lover of dark chocolate, outdoor adventures, and celebrating the uniqueness of every culture!

About the Artist

The artwork found throughout this book are original pieces created by our very own HserKu. One of the incredible women of Braverly, she has been with us from opening day at our café, and we would not be where we are without her faithfulness, courage, and gifts. HserKu, thank you for using what's in your hand to give the Father glory and bring these stories to life. May you continue to courageously step into the place the Lord has created for you and may your brave steps influence others to take their own courageous journey.

Resources

No matter where we find ourselves on our journey with the Father, we need trusted voices to speak truth into our lives. These have been powerful voices and messages that have shaped our journeys, and our hope is that they will encourage and challenge you as well.

If you have never accepted the love, grace, life, and truth of Jesus, we would encourage you to start there. It's okay to come to the table with lots of questions and hesitancy. This is why the church exists—to walk alongside one another toward the Father and to help point people to Jesus. If you want to learn more about following Jesus or are ready to follow Him, we would encourage you to connect with a church in your town, a trusted Christian friend, or connect with us on our website www.aplacecalledbraverly. com. We'd love to answer any questions you have or direct you to a local church who can come alongside you.

For a full and updated list of resources, visit our website www.aplacecalledbraverly.com/resources.

Friends, let's dive in—read, listen, share with friends, and step a little closer to your heavenly Father who longs to share more of His heart with you!

Chapter 1: Resting in the Father's Extravagant Love
- Podcast: *Discovering the Father's Heart* by Jonathan David and Melissa Helser
- Article: *A Palestinian Perspective on the Prodigal Son* by Rev. Dr. Daniel DeForest London

Chapter 2: He Calls Me Daughter
- Podcast: *The Voice that Defines You* by Jonathan David and Melissa Helser
- Book: *The Supernatural Ways of Royalty* by Kris Vallotton and Bill Johnson
- Song: *You Say* by Lauren Daigle
- Song: *Who You Say I Am* by Hillsong Worship

Chapter 3: He Calls Me Courageous
- Song: *Take Courage (Live)* by Bethel Music & Kristene DiMarco
- Song: *You Make Me Brave (Live)* by Bethel Music & Amanda Cook
- Podcast: *Called to Courage* by Kris Vallotton
- Book: *The Barbarian Way* by Erwin McManus

Chapter 4: He Created a Place for Me
- Book: *Fashioned to Reign* by Kris Vallotton
- Book: *Jesus Feminist* by Sarah Bessey

- Book: *Half of the Church* by Carolyn Curtis James
- Podcast: *The Original Women's Liberation Movement* by Kris Vallotton

Chapter 5: He Calls Us to Surrender

- Book: *Birthing the Miraculous* by Heidi Baker
- Podcast: *Friendship with the Holy Spirit* by Jonathan David and Melissa Helser
- Podcast: *Leaning into the Holy Spirit* by Jonathan David and Melissa Helser
- Song: *Communion* by Maverick City Music (feat. Steffany Gretzinger)
- Song: *Abraham* by Josh Baldwin
- Song: *Promises* by Maverick City Music (feat. Joe L Barnes & Naomi Raine)
- Song: *Every Table is an Altar* by Jason Upton

Chapter 6: He Asks Us, "What's that in Your Hand?"

- Song: *Anything is Possible (Live)* by Bethel Music & Dante Bowe
- Book: *I Am Not But I Know I Am: Welcome to the Story of God* by Louie Giglio

Chapter 7: Your Story Matters

- Song: *Out of Hiding* by Steffany Gretzinger
- Song: *The Story I'll Tell* by Maverick City Music (feat. Naomi Raine)
- Book: *Daring Greatly* by Brene Brown
- Book: *Rising Strong* by Brene Brown

- Book: *Unashamed* by Christine Caine
- Podcast: *The Power of Instead: Part 1 & 2* by Jonathan David and Melissa Helser

Chapter 8: Courageous Communion

- Song: *Communion* by Maverick City Music
- Book: *Love Does* by Bob Goff
- Book: *Everybody Always* by Bob Goff
- Book: *Imperfect Courage* by Jessica Honegger
- Book: *The Four Loves* by C.S. Lewis
- Podcast: *Friendship with the Holy Spirit* by Jonathan David and Melissa Helser
- Podcast: *Leaning into the Holy Spirit* by Jonathan David and Melissa Helser
- Podcast: *Growing Roots* by Jonathan David and Melissa Helser

Endnotes

1   Romans 3:23

2   Romans 5:8; 6:23

3   Romans 10:9-10

4   Matthew 28:19-20

5   Ephesians 3:10; John 15:16

6   Jeremiah 29:13

7   Jonathan Helser, "Unlocking Your Identity," September 6, 2018, in *Jonathan and Melissa Helser Podcast*, podcast, MP3 audio, 30:24, https://www.jonathanhelser.com/packages/

8   Daniel DeForest London, "A Palestinian Perspective on the Prodigal Son," *Daniel DeForest London* (blog), March 14, 2010, https://deforestlondon.wordpress.com/2010/03/14/a-palestinian-perspective-on-the-prodigal-son/

9   2 Corinthians 10:5b

10   Psalm 149:4

11   1 Peter 2:9

12   1 John 3:1

13   John 14:27

14   1 John 4:7-11

15   John 6:35; 8:12; 10:11

16   Sleeping At Last, "Saturn", Tom Shea & Michael
     Means, LatinAutor-PeerMusic, Audiam (label &
     publishing), June 28, 2016, YouTube, 4:49 minutes,
     youtube.com/watch?v=dzNvk80XY9s

17   Kris Vallotton, "The Original Women's Liberation
     Movement," Septmber 10. 2021, in *The Kris Vallot-
     ton Podcast*, podcast, MP3 audio, 1:19:13, https://
     www.krisvallotton.com/womens-liberation

18   Luke 10:40, TPT

19   Luke 10:41-42, TPT

20   Luke 10:42, TPT

21   Heidi Baker, "Knowing the Ways of God", Grace
     Center, September 9, 2014, YouTube, 1:05:28 min-
     utes, youtube.com/watch?v=FuEVWzZwodY

22   Exodus 4:13

23   G2842 - koinōnia - Strong's Greek Lexicon (kjv),"
     Blue Letter Bible, Accessed May 6, 2020, https://
     www.blueletterbible.org/lexicon/g2842/kjv/tr/0-1/

24   Mark 14:36, NLT

25   Mark 14:36, NLT

26   C.S. Lewis, *The Four Loves* (New York: Harcourt,
     Brace, Jovanovich, 1960), 169.

27   Luke 23:34, NLT

A free ebook edition is available with the purchase of this book.

To claim your free ebook edition:

1. Visit MorganJamesBOGO.com
2. Sign your name CLEARLY in the space
3. Complete the form and submit a photo of the entire copyright page
4. You or your friend can download the ebook to your preferred device

Print & Digital Together Forever.

Snap a photo   Free ebook   Read anywhere

CPSIA information can be obtained
at www.ICGtesting.com
Printed in the USA
JSHW052107020622
26627JS00003B/5